# Hip Crochet

# NATALIE CLEGG

NEW
HOLLAND

First published 2013 by
New Holland Publishers Pty Ltd
London • Sydney • Cape Town • Auckland

Garfield House, 86–88 Edgware Road, London, W2 2EA, United Kingdom
Wembley Square, First Floor, Solan Road, Gardens, Cape Town, 8001, South Africa
1/66 Gibbes Street, Chatswood, NSW, 2067, Australia
218 Lake Road, Northcote, Auckland, New Zealand

www.newhollandpublishers.com

A record of this book is held at the British Library

ISBN 9781780090559

Publisher: Fiona Schultz
Publishing director: Lliane Clarke
Senior editor: Simona Hill
Designer: Tracy Loughlin
Proofreader: Melanie Hibbert
Photographs: Location photography by Jon Meade. Still lifes by Graeme Gillies. Technique photographs taken by Mark Winwood. Photograph page 153 taken by the author.
Production director: Olga Dementiev
Printer: Toppan Leefung China Ltd.

10 9 8 7 6 5 4 3 2 1

Keep up with New Holland Publishers on Facebook http://www.facebook.com/NewHollandPublishers

# Contents

# Introduction

Furnishing your home with crocheted items that express your creativity and personality is deeply satisfying. You have the pleasure of deciding upon a project, choosing the yarn and the colourscheme, planning the making and the project's final use and then carefully crafting the item. The projects that feature in this lovely book are tactile, colourful, functional and decorative, but above all they have a strong sense of design as well as an element of fun. Each is designed to enhance your home environment by adding a splash of colour and individuality.

The colours I have chosen are deliberately bright, bold and funky, challenging you to be brave. The designs draw inspiration from the '60s and '70s while offering a contemporary take on crochet. The projects encompass many methods of working including lace, motifs, amigurumi, and even the humble granny square. Some of the designs have written patterns, and some have charts.

Each item has been designed to push your skill as a crochet maker, though there are projects included that are suitable for a beginner. The patterns have been designed to be efficient and variations are provided for many so that you can extend the concepts and innovate your own designs.

Crochet is the easiest and quickest needlework skill to learn but with the widest range of possibilities. The key to successful crochet is to read the pattern thoroughly, relax and enjoy the process of making as much as achieving the finished item. This book is designed to encompass as much of the fun it is possible to find in crochet so that you too can make happy hip crochet.

Enjoy.

*Natalie C.*

# Crochet Basics

Crochet is a needlework skill using a hook and yarn. The yarn is looped around the hook in a set or series of combinations to create various effects. To make the fabric from the yarn each row of loops acts as a foundation for the next row or round. The different stitches and their textured effects are beautiful. There is always one loop left on the hook at the end of each stitch. Errors quickly become evident and it is easy to pull the work back to fix it.

There are several methods of working crochet including:

• **In the round** (see Zing Bedcover) A piece is worked in a round and joined after the last stitch to the first with a slip stitch. The work then continues to the next row.

• **In rows** The project being worked is turned over at the end of each row (see Country Flower Cushion).

• **Amigurumi** is a Japanese style of crocheting small figures using a series of increases and decreases to create shapes. **Amigurumi techniques** are used in two ways. Some of the beads made in the Bead Door Curtain are made with each row joined at the end. In the Hot Chilli Ristra and String the rows continue in a spiral. It is important to count the stitches and use stitch markers to keep track. With amigurumi the wrong side of the work is the finished side.

• **The Jacquard crochet method** is also included. In this technique a multi-coloured design is worked and the threads are carried behind the work. The Union Jack Cushion includes this technique.

• Two of the projects are **felted**. They are crocheted using wool that will felt when washed vigorously in a washing machine. The effect of washing shrinks the wool and creates an interesting chunky effect. (See Aquarius Floormat).

• Another method used in some projects is known as **join-as-you-go**. Instead of making lots of different elements and stitching them together at the end, it is possible to join pieces as the work is crocheted. The Gypsy Cascade Tablecloth is an example of this.

## TERMINOLOGY, ABBREVIATIONS AND SYMBOLS

The patterns are all written using English crochet terminology and abbreviations. The table on the following page gives the abbreviations used in this book as well as the American equivalents.

Some of the patterns are charted using standard symbols. Special pattern stitches are sometimes used in a project and are explained at the beginning of each pattern and the relevant abbreviation is given for that pattern.

# CROCHET TERMS AND ABBREVIATIONS

| Abbreviation | UK Stitch Term | Symbol | US Term | US Abbreviation |
|---|---|---|---|---|
| beg | Beginning | | | |
| ch | Chain | ○ | | |
| cl | Cluster | ⚇ | | CL |
| cm | Centimetre | | | |
| dc | Double crochet | × | Single crochet | sc |
| dec | Decrease | | | |
| dtr | Double treble | ‡ | Treble | Tr |
| fc | Foundation chain | | | |
| g | Gram | | | |
| hk | Hook | | | |
| htr | Half treble crochet | T | Half double crochet | hdc |
| in | Inch | | | |
| inc | Increase | | | |
| lp | Loop | | | |
| oz | Ounce | | | |
| pc | Picot | | | |
| rev dc | Reverse double crochet | | Reverse single crochet | Rev sc |
| sk | Skip | | | |
| sl st | Slip stitch | • | | |
| sp | Space | | | |
| st | Stitch | | | |
| tog | Together | | | |
| tr | Treble | ‡ | Double crochet | Dc |
| ttr | Triple treble | | Double treble | dtr |
| yo | Yarn over | | | |

*These stitches may be made using dc or tr and may have a number of different legs as indicated in the symbol. In some crochet books this stitch is called a bobble stitch.

## READING CHARTS

Once you get used to looking at and working with charts they become very easy. Essentially all the crochet charts in this book are for motif-based items.

The chart is a graphic representation of what the finished item will look like. Start in the centre and read the pattern in the round from right to left (anti-clockwise); the same direction that you work in. Finding the beginning and end of each row is sometimes challenging, so look for the beginning chains and the joining slip stitches.

The best way to learn to read charts is to practise on one of the easier patterns such as the Aquarius Floormat where both a chart and a written pattern have been given. With practice you should become familiar with them.

One thing that is not always clearly indicated on a crochet chart is whether to work into the stitch or into a ring/loop or chain stitch. Follow common practice. Usually when a ring or a loop or a chain space is formed you should crochet the next row into the ring/loop/space and not into the individual chain stitches.

**Tip** Left-handed crocheters work in the opposite way and may find it easier to trace the pattern onto tracing paper and then read it from the other side.

## JACQUARD CROCHET DIAGRAMS

The diagrams given show one block for each stitch. Start to read the pattern at the bottom of the diagram and work upwards making the colour changes as shown. Row numbers have been inserted to help you find your way. The first row begins on the right-hand side of the diagram and you work the row from right to left. You then turn the work and following the diagram from the left work the colour changes specified.

The shape of the finished design will alter if you decide to use the chart with a different size stitch.

## SKILL LEVEL

The patterns in this book assume that you have some knowledge of crochet, but don't be put off if you're a beginner. The projects and patterns have been designed to be as simple as possible while using a wide range of techniques. Even the new crocheter will find the projects straightforward and fun to make.

It is important to skim-read each pattern through before you start so that you gain an understanding of what is required. Each pattern sets out the type of yarns or threads as well as other materials used and also explains which hook size you need.

## TENSION

With each pattern the finished size of the item or motif is given. Sometimes the size is important for the project and if this is the case a tension guide is given. Sizes are given in metric and imperial.

Every crocheter is different and a number

of variables including yarn, hook size, tension and crocheting style, can affect the size and shape of the finished item.

Work a sample piece first and adjust your hook, yarn or the pattern, if you are able, so that you can match the tension.

Note that your tension will adjust once you start a new project and it may be helpful to crochet for a while on a smaller hook before beginning the project.

## UNDERSTANDING REPEATING PATTERN INSTRUCTIONS

Many patterns have repeating instructions that may be denoted in two ways.

In example 1 the instructions within the brackets should be repeated the number of times as indicated.

**Example 1** *Row 5: Ch 1; dc in same sp as joining; (ch 4, dc into top of cl, ch 4, dc into next tr) 15 times; ch 4; dc into top of tr; ch 4. Join with sl st to first dc [32 4ch lps].*

In example 2, the pattern instructions have an asterisk, which denotes a repeat. Initially the asterisk is ignored and you should continue to follow the pattern instructions until referred back to the asterisk.

**Example 2** *Row 5: Ch 1, dc in same sps joining; \*Ch 4; dc into top of cl; ch 4; dc into next tr. Repeat from \* 14 more times; ch 4; dc into top of tr; ch 4. Join with sl st to first dc [32 4ch lps].*

In both examples the end result is exactly the same.

# Tools and Materials

Ensure you have all the tools and materials to hand before beginning a project.

## NOTEBOOK

It may seem strange to have a notebook as the first thing on the list but keeping a record of your work will save you a great deal of frustration if you have to come back to a project after setting it aside for a while.

When starting a new project, record the name, type, colour and batch numbers of the yarn to be used, the hook size you have chosen, and any adjustments you have decided to make to the pattern. It's always nice to have a record of the date you started. Also take a photograph of the finished item and glue that in your notebook in case you ever want to make the project again.

## HOOKS

Crochet hooks range in size from 0.4 mm to very large. They are made in a variety of materials though smaller hooks are usually made of steel; medium hooks are often aluminium; and large hooks may be plastic. Some have soft grip handles. Choosing a hook is a personal choice.

A small hook is used with thicker yarn for the amigurumi-style projects. The effect is to provide a stiffer finish with smaller holes in the fabric. A large hook with a fine thread will provide a soft, lacy effect often seen in shawls and scarves. Sometimes a yarn may split, this problem can be quite acute with some yarns, and can often be overcome by choosing a hook with a sharper tip. It's a good idea to build up a collection of hooks before finding the one that fits the project requirements. Once you start a project, use the same hook throughout.

### Hook Conversion Chart

There are two sizing options for hooks and the chart opposite will help you to convert to the metric system as used in this book. New hooks in the UK are metric but if you collect old or vintage hooks you will come across many with the old-style UK measurements so they are included in the chart opposite.

## SCISSORS

A small sharp pair of good quality needlework scissors is essential for cutting off woven-in yarn ends. Never use them to cut paper, which will blunt them.

## HOOK CONVERSION CHART

| Metric mm | US (Closest equivalent) | UK |
|---|---|---|
| 0.4 | - | - |
| 0.6 | | 6 Steel |
| .75 | 14 Steel | 5 |
| 1 | 12 | 4 |
| 1.25 | | 3 |
| 1.5 | 8 | 2 ½ |
| 1.75 | 6 | 2 |
| 2 | 0 Standard | 14 Standard |
| 2.5 | 1½ | 12 |
| 3 | 2½ | 11 |
| 3.25 | D/3 | 10 |
| 3.5 | E/4 | 9 |
| 4 | F/5 | 8 |
| 4.5 | G/6 | 7 |
| 5 | H/8 | 6 |
| 5.5 | I/9 | 5 |
| 6 | J/10 | 4 |
| 7 | K/10.25 | 2 |
| 8 | L/11 | 0 |
| 9 | M/13 | 00 |
| 10 | N/15 | 000 |
| 12 | 17 | |
| 15 | P/Q/19 | |

## WOOL AND TAPESTRY SEWING NEEDLES

Needles are used for weaving in the yarn ends. Normally these are blunt-tipped with large eyes. It is useful to keep a variety of sizes. For very thick yarn it is possible to get aluminium needles with large resin loop eyes that are easy to thread. Finer tapestry needles work well for weaving in ends on fine thread projects such as the Snowflake Hanging.

## TAPE MEASURE AND RULER

A dressmaking tape measure is essential as is a standard 30 cm (12 in) ruler.

## OTHER USEFUL ITEMS

**Pompom Makers** that are made of plastic can be used repeatedly and are much easier to use than making cardboard rings.
**Wool Pins** are long pins with flat heads. They are not as stiff as dressmaking pins and sit well in the wool yarn.
**Stitch Markers** are inserted to mark a particular stitch so you can keep count in projects that are worked continuously, or to keep your place when increasing/decreasing. Alternatively, you can use a piece of contrasting thread and tie it into the work as a stitch marker.
**T-shaped Pins** are used mainly for blocking.

## ABOUT YARNS

A very wide range of yarns made from different materials and in different weights (known as ply) has been used for the projects in this book.

It is always great fun to experiment with different yarns, but the ones chosen for the projects presented here have been based on the desired effect of the design so any

yarn substitution that you make should be undertaken with care.

Weights of yarn can differ substantially between manufacturers and indeed some yarns appear to be thinner/thicker if in another colour. So, an Aran-weight yarn made by one company may be similar to a Double Knitting (DK)-weight from another company.

A Yarn Index is provided at the back of the book which lists all the yarns used. This also presents a 'wraps per inch' measurement (WPI) to help you, should you wish to substitute the yarn. Alternative yarns will not always work in the same way even if they are made from the same materials and have similar WPIs.

In each of the patterns, yardage and weight of each ball has been given, but if your crocheting style is firmer you may find you use more yarn. If you want to test yardage make a swatch in the main pattern stitch and weigh it. (Electronic kitchen scales work really well for this.) You can then recalculate yardage because you will have the proportions of weight to yardage from the yarn used in the pattern. (Cotton yarns are heavier than acrylic so the yardage on a 50 g (1¾ oz) ball is much less for cotton than for acrylic even if both are DK.)

## TOP TIPS FOR SUCCESSFUL CROCHETING

- Wherever possible crochet over ends. Weave in ends properly (See Techniques).
- If you are crocheting too stiffly, pull the thread on your little finger forward to cover the main knuckle on the finger.
- At the end of each stitch only one loop is left on the hook.
- Always make a test piece to check your tension where appropriate.
- Understand what a stitch looks like from the front and the back, then you'll know when you are working into the correct part of the stitch.
- In starting a piece of work the slip knot used is not the first chain.
- A slip stitch is not a structural stitch, it is used to move from one place to another in a pattern, or for top stitching, or to create tension and stiffness.
- Always use the same hook from start to finish for the project.
- Always use every bit of yarn, and don't throw any away until you are sure you will have enough.
- Check the quantities you need and try to ensure you can get more of the same colour batch. Keep the yarn labels.
- Always write down what changes you have made to the pattern, such as different yarn, hook size and so on.
- Experiment, try different yarns and colours. Try the variations given for the patterns or try your own.

Tools and Materials

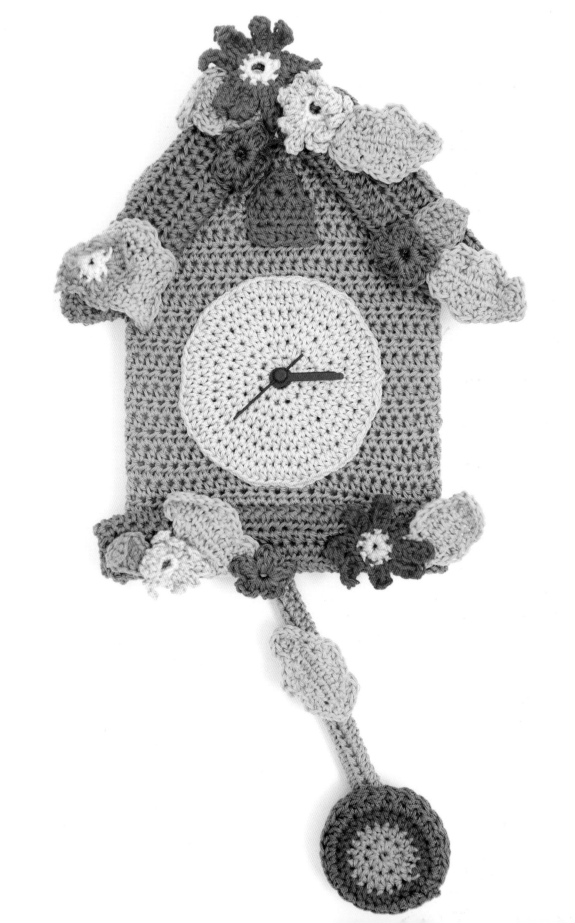

# THE PROJECTS

# ZING BEDCOVER

A little bit decadent, this bedcover is made from coloured doilies in a wool-mix yarn. The pattern calls for a join-as-you-go method with smaller motifs added as fillers between the larger motifs. The bedcover is very stretchy and, in this lovely soft yarn, will drape beautifully.

## MATERIALS
**Yarn**: Sirdar Country Style DK, 100 g (3½ oz)
- 4 x Dusky pink, col no 423 (D pink)
- 4 x Cream, col no 411 (Cream)
- 3 x Rosehip, col no 527 (B pink)
- 3 x Flutter, col no 601 (Lilac)
- 3 x Apples, col no 599 (Green)
- 3 x Mountain ash, col no 589 (Ash)
- 1 x Damson, col no 604 (Damson)

Wool sewing needle
Scissors
**Hook**: 4 mm

## TENSION
Using a 4 mm hook the first 5 rows of the motif measures 13.5 cm (5 in). A finished motif measures 30 cm (12 in) diameter.

## FINISHED SIZE
The bedspread is 6 motifs deep and 7 motifs wide. It measures 1.8 x 2.1 m (71 x 83 in). This bedspread is very stretchy and it will expand the more it is used.

## SPECIAL PATTERN STITCHES

**Dtrcl = Double treble cluster**: Make 4 dtrs but leave the last lp of each dtr on the hk, yo and pull through all 5 lps on the hk.

**Beg dtrcl = Beginning double treble cluster**: Ch 3 (counts as first dtr), make 3 dtrs, leaving the last lp of each dtr on the hk, yo and pull through all 5 lps on the hk.

**Trcl= Treble cluster**: Make 3 trs, but leave the last lp of each tr on the hk, yo and pull through all 4 lps on the hk.

**Beg trcl = Beginning treble cluster**: Ch 2 (counts a first tr), make 2 tr, leaving the last lp of each tr on hk, yarn over and pull through 4 lps on hk.

## PATTERN – MAIN MOTIF

The pattern is given here as a chart as well as a written pattern. There are 9 rows to the Main Motif and 3 rows for the Filler Motif. You will ned to make 42 motifs according to the Motif Colour Chart. The Layout Diagram gives the corresponding position of each motif. The motifs are joined as work progresses. The filler motifs are made last and inserted once the main motifs are in place. (See Techniques for more detail on the join-as-you-go method.)

Ch 7. Join with sl st to form a ring.

**Row 1**: Into ring work as follows: beg dtrcl; (ch 5, trcl, ch 5, dtrcl) 3 times; ch 5, trcl; ch 5. Join with sl st to top of beg dtrcl [8 5ch lps].

**Row 2**: Sl st in each of next 2 ch and into 5ch lp; dc into same lp; (ch 7, dc into next 5ch sp) 7 times; ch 7. Join with sl st into first dc [8 7ch lps].

**Row 3**: Ch 1, dc in same sp as joining; (ch 4, dc into 7ch lp, ch 4, dc into next dc) 7 times; ch 4; dc into next 7ch lp; ch 4. Join with sl st into first dc [16 4ch lps].

**Row 4**: Ch 5 (counts as 1 tr and 2 ch); (trcl into next 4ch lp, ch 2, 1 tr into next dc, ch 2) 15 times; trcl into next 4ch lp; ch 2. Join with sl st to second ch of beg ch 4 [16trcls].

**Row 5**: Ch 1, dc in same sp as joining; (ch 4, dc into top of cl, ch 4, dc into tr) 15 times; ch 4, dc into top of cl, ch 4. Join with sl st to first dc [32 4ch lps].

**Row 6**: Sl st into first 4ch lp; 1 ch, 2 dc into same sp; * work (1 dc, 1 htr, 1 tr, 1 dtr) into next 4ch lp; work (1 dtr, 1 tr, 1 htr, 1 dc) into next 4ch lp**; 2 dc into each of the next 2 4ch lps. Repeat from * 6 more times; repeat from * to ** once; 2 dc into the next 4ch lps. Join with sl st to the first dc.

**Row 7**: Rev dc into the sp between first dc and last dc of previous row; *ch 5; into sp between the next 2 dtrs from previous row work (1 tr, ch 2) 3 times, 1 tr into same sp; ch 5; work dc between middle of 6 dc grouping from previous row. Rep from * 6 more times; into sp between the 2 two dtrs from previous row work (1 tr, ch 2) 3 times,

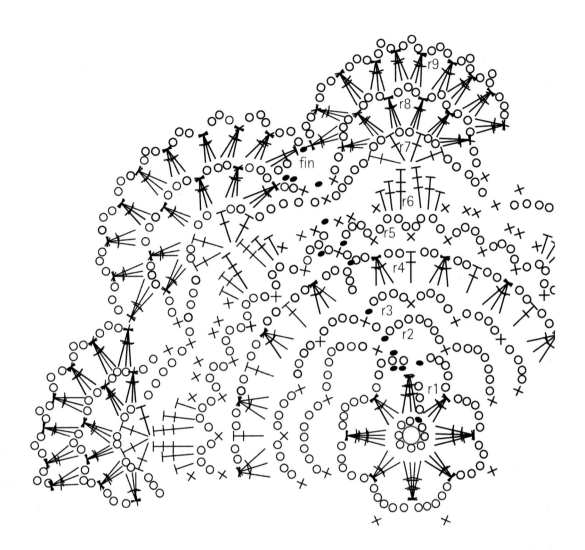

1 tr into same sp, ch 5. Join with sl st to first dc.

**Row 8**: Sl st into 5ch lp, ch 1, 1 dc into same lp; ch 2; *into next 2ch sp work (trcl, ch 3, trcl), (shell made); (ch 3, shell into next 2ch sp) twice; ch 2; 1 dc into next 5ch lp; ** 1 dc into next 5ch lp; ch 2. Rep from * 6 more times. Repeat from * to ** once. Join with sl st to first dc.

**Row 9**: Sl st into next dc, and into each of the next 2 ch, sl st into top of trcl; sl st into 3ch sp; (beg trcl into 3ch sp (counts as a trcl), ch 3, trcl), (shell made); (ch 3, shell into next 3ch sp) 4 times; * shell into 3ch sp; (ch 3, shell into next 3ch sp) 4 times. Rep from * 6 more times. Join with sl st to top of beg trcl.

**Joining Main Motifs instructions for row 9**

In row 8 there are 8 'bunches' of clusters

with ch lps between. The join is made when you get to the middle 3ch lp of each bunch. Make ch 1, join with a dc into the opposite lp and ch 1. Continue with the trcl. Two joins are made to the motif to the left, and two joins to the motif above.

## FILLER MOTIFS

Make 30. Insert these motifs after you have joined the surrounding Main Motifs. Follow pattern for Main Motif to row 3. From this row you will skip the first and last unused 3ch lps of each of the bunches of the main motifs and join 4 times into each of the adjoined motifs.

**Row 4**: Ch 1; sl st into next ch and into 4ch lp; ch 1, dc into same sp; (ch 4, join with a dc into adjoining motif, ch 4, dc into 4ch lp of filler motif) 16 times, joining with a sl st into the beg dc at the end. Fasten off. Weave in all ends.

## BLOCKING

Dampen this bedspread well. Peg it out on the floor and stretch it evenly. Allow to dry. Alternatively steam block the bedspread but take care as there is a high acrylic content in the yarn.

## VARIATION

This pattern is seminine and can be used in a lot of ways. A lovely tablecloth could be made using fine cotton thread.

## COLOUR CHART

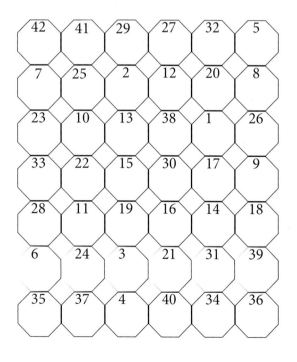

Zing Bedcover

# MOTIF COLOUR CHART

| Motif no | Colourway | Colourway |
|---|---|---|
| | Rows 1–9 | |
| 1 | Green | |
| 2 | Lilac | |
| 3 | D Pink | |
| 4 | Ash | |
| | | |
| | Rows 1–4 | Rows 5–9 |
| 5 | Green | D Pink |
| 6 | Lilac | Green |
| 7 | Ash | D Pink |
| 8 | Ash | Cream |
| 9 | Cream | Green |
| 10 | Cream | Lilac |
| 11 | Cream | D Pink |
| 12 | Cream | B Pink |
| 13 | Damson | Cream |
| 14 | Damson | Ash |
| 15 | B Pink | Ash |
| 16 | B Pink | D Pink |
| 17 | D Pink | Cream |
| 18 | D Pink | Lilac |
| | | |
| | Rows 1–7 | Rows 8–9 |
| 19 | Lilac | Green |
| 20 | D Pink | Lilac |
| 21 | Cream | Ash |
| 22 | Ash | Damson |
| 23 | Green | B Pink |

| Motif no | Colourway | Colourway | Colourway |
|---|---|---|---|
| | Rows 1–3 | Rows 4–9 | |
| 24 | Ash | Cream | |
| 25 | B Pink | Green | |
| 26 | B Pink | Lilac | |
| 27 | Lilac | Green | |
| 28 | Green | Ash | |
| 29 | Cream | D Pink | |
| 30 | Cream | Lilac | |
| | | | |
| | Rows 1–3 | Row 4 | Rows 5–9 |
| 31 | Green | Cream | Lilac |
| 32 | Cream | B Pink | Ash |
| 33 | Lilac | Damson | Cream |
| 34 | B Pink | Ash | D Pink |
| 35 | B Pink | Green | Ash |
| 36 | Damson | Lilac | Green |
| 37 | Damson | Ash | D Pink |
| | | | |
| | Rows 1–3 | Rows 4–7 | Rows 8–9 |
| 38 | Lilac | Green | Ash |
| 39 | Green | B Pink | D Pink |
| 40 | B Pink | D Pink | Lilac |
| 41 | Damson | Ash | Cream |
| 42 | B Pink | Cream | Green |

# Black Cat Doorstop

A little bit cheeky, this lucky cat will guard your door. An amigurumi technique is used to make this doorstop, which is quick to make. Instructions are also given for a colourful collar complete with flower.

## MATERIALS

**Yarn**: Stylecraft Special DK, 100 g (3½ oz)
- Black, col no 1002 (Black)
- Matador, col no 1010 (Red)
- Sunshine, col no 1114 (Yellow)
- Violet, col no 1277 (Violet)

Wool sewing needle

Scissors

2 Chenille pipe cleaners

Stuffing

400 g (14 oz) aquarium pebbles

2 vintage buttons [for eyes]

1 brass bell

1 pencil or dowel about 20 cm (8 in) long

1 pair of black stockings or tights

**Hook**: 3.5 mm

## TENSION

Tension is not important in this project.

## FINISHED SIZE

The cat is about 30 cm (12 in) tall, but will be a little shorter once the stuffing settles

## SPECIAL PATTERN STITCHES

**Htrdec = Half treble decrease**: Yo, insert hk into next st, yo, pull through, yo, insert hk into following st, yo, pull through, yo and pull through all 5 lps on hk (decrease made).

**Dc2tog = Double crochet decrease** Insert hk into specified st, yo and draw through, insert hk into next st, yo and draw through, yo and draw through all 3 lps on hk (decrease made).

## PATTERN

The cat is made from the base upwards in a continual spiral, the rows are not joined. It is stitched closed at the top. The tail and collar embellishment are added later. This amigurumi pattern is unusual since it uses half treble (htr) instead of a double crochet (dc) as the main stitch. The wrong side of the work will be the visible side.

## CAT BODY AND HEAD

In black, ch 26 loosely.

**Foundation row**: 1 htr into third ch from hk; 1 htr in each of next 20 ch. Into third ch from end work 2 htr; into penultimate ch from end work 2 htr; into last ch work 4 htr. Rotate the work (do not turn) and continue working into the unused lps of the beg ch; work 2 htr into each of the next 2 lps; work 1 htr into each of the next 19 lps; 2 htr into each of the next 2 lps; work 4 htr into unused ch, work 2 htr into each of the next 2 htr. Place a stitch marker into the last htr made – this indicates the end of the row [64htr]. (The first 2 htr made at the beginning do not count.)

**Row 1**: 1 htr into next 19 htr; (2 htr into next htr; 1 htr into next htr) 6 times)) twice. Move stitch marker to last htr [74htr].

**Row 2**: (1 htr into next 19 htr; 2 htr into next htr; 1 htr into each of next 16 htr; 2 htr into next htr) twice. [78htr].

**Row 3**: 1 htr into each htr [78htr].

**Row 4**: (2 htr into next htr; 1 htr in each of next 38 htr) twice [80htr].

**Rows 5–6**: 1 htr into each htr [80htr].

**Row 7**: (1 htr into each of next 8 htr, htr2tog) 8 times [72htr].

**Rows 8–10**: 1 htr into each htr [72htr].

**Row 11**: 1 htr into each of the next 60 htr; htr2tog; 1 htr into each of next 4 htr; htr2tog; 1 htr into each of next 4 htr [70htr].

**Row 12**: (1 htr into each of the next 4 htr; htr2tog) twice; 1 htr into each of the next 58 htr [68htr].

**Row 13**: 1 htr into each of the next 56 htr; (htr2tog; 1 htr into each of the next 4 htr) twice [66htr].

**Row 14**: (1 htr into each of the next 4 htr; htr2tog) twice, 1 htr into each of next 54 htr [64htr].

**Row 15**: 1 htr into each htr [64htr].

**Row 16**: 1 htr into each of the next 52 htr; (htr2tog; 1 htr into each of the next 2 htr) three times [61htr].

**Row 17**: (1 htr into each of the next 2 htr; htr2tog) three times; 1 htr into each of next 49 htr [58htr].

**Row 18**: 1 htr into each htr [58htr].

**Row 19**: 1 htr into each of the next 46 htr; (htr2tog; 1 htr into each of the next 2 htr) three times [55htr].

**Row 20**: (1 htr into each of the next 2 htr; htr2tog) three times; 1 htr into each of the next 43 htr [52htr].

**Row 21**: 1 htr into each htr [52htr].

**Row 22**: 1 htr into each of the next 40 htr; htr2tog twice; (1 htr into each of the next 2 htr) twice; 1 htr into each of the next 2 htr [48htr].

**Row 23**: (1 htr into each of the next 2 htr; htr2tog twice) twice; 1 htr into each of the next 7 htr; htr2tog twice; 1 htr into each of the next 4 htr; htr2tog twice; 1 htr into each of the next 17 htr [40htr].

**Rows 24–25**: 1 htr into each htr [40htr].

**Row 26**: 1 htr into each of the next 3 htr; htr2tog; (1 htr into each of the next 6 htr; htr2tog) four times; 1 htr into each of the next 3 htr [35htr].

## Neck Shaping

**Row 27**: 1 htr into each of next 3 htr; htr2tog 3 times; (1 htr into each of next 3 htr; htr2tog twice) twice; 1 htr into each of next 3 htr; htr2tog 3 times; 1 htr into each of next 3 htr [25htr].

**Rows 28–30**: 1 htr into each htr [25htr].

## Head Shaping

**Row 31**: 1 htr into each of next 2 htr; 2 htr into each of the next 3 htr; 1 htr in each of next 4 htr; 2 htr into each of the next 3 htr; 1 htr in each of next 2 htr; 2 htr into each of the next 2 htr; 1 htr in each of next 5 htr; 2 htr into each of the next 2 htr; 1 htr in each of next 2 htr [35htr].

**Row 32**: 1 htr into each htr [35htr].

**Row 33**: 2 htr into the next htr; 1 htr into next htr; 2 htr into next htr; 1 htr into each of next 2 htr; 2 htr into next htr; 1 htr into next htr; 2 htr into next htr; 1 htr in each of next 11 htr; 2 htr into next htr; 1 htr into next htr; 2 htr into next htr; 1 htr in each of next 2 htr; 2 htr into next htr; 1 htr into next htr; 2 htr into next htr; 1 htr in each of next 8 htr [43htr].

**Rows 34–36**: 1 htr into each htr [43htr].

**Row 37**: 1 htr into each of the next 4 htr; htr2tog twice; 1 htr into next htr; htr2tog; 1 htr into next htr; htr2tog twice; 1 htr into each of the next 3 htr; htr2tog; 1 htr into next htr; htr2 tog; 1 htr into each of the next 3 htr; htr2tog twice; 1 htr into next htr; htr2tog; 1 htr into next htr; htr2tog twice; 1 htr into each of the next 4 htr [31htr].

**Rows 38–40**: 1 htr into each htr [31htr].

## Ear Shaping

**Row 41**: (Ch 2 after turning counts as a htr.) 1 htr into each of the next 26 htr; turn work; ch 2; 1 htr into each of the next 8 htr. Place a stitch marker in the last htr; turn; ch 2; sk 1 htr; 1 htr into each of the next 7 htr;

each of the next 28 sts [29htr]; make 5 htr into next st; make 1 htr in each of the next 7 ch; 1 dc in each of next 6 ch. Turn.

**Row 2**: Ch 1; 1 dc into each of next 10 dc; 1 htr into next 36 htr [47 sts total]. Turn.

**Row 3**: Ch 2; 1 htr into next 29 htr; 1 dc into next 14 dc; sl st into each of last 3 sts. Turn.

**Row 4**: This is the joining row and will make the tail twist. Double piece over and make the following sts going through the double V of the last row and into the free lps of the foundation ch: sl st into next 5 sts; dc into next 4 sts; dc2tog 5 times; dc into next 11 sts; htr into last 22 stitches. Fasten off. Leave a long tail for sewing up and to attach to the cat.

## COLLAR

Ch 32.

**Row 1**: 1 htr into second ch from hk and into each ch across. Fasten off, leaving a long thread to sew collar to cat.

## RUFFLE FLOWER

**Row 1**: With yellow, ch 3; 4 htr into third ch from hk. Join with sl st to third ch of beg 3ch.

**Row 2**: Ch 2 (counts as 1 htr); 1 htr into same sp as joining; 2 htr into each htr. Join with sl st to beg 2 ch [10htr]. Fasten off.

**Row 3**: With violet, join into any st; ch 2; (2 tr, 1 htr, 1 dc) into the same st; (1 htr, 2 tr, 1 htr, 1 dc) into each htr round [10 petals]. Join with sl st to base of beg 2ch. Fasten off, leaving a long thread to sew flower to collar.

turn; ch 2; 1 htr into each of the next 6 htr**; sl st across the ear and down to the htr with the stitch marker; 1 htr into each of the next 17 htr; repeat from * to **. Fasten off. (It is not necessary to use a stitch marker on the repeat.)

## Tail

In this part of the pattern the ch 1 and ch 2 at the beg of each row count as a main st. Ch 44.

**Row 1**: Htr in the third ch from hk and in

## MAKING UP

**1**   Pin the collar in place around the neck of the cat. Position the join to the left-hand side. Sew collar to main body attaching the bell about 2 cm (¾ in) to the right of the join.

**2**   Weave in yarn ends of flower centre. Sew flower to the collar over the collar join. Weave in ends.

**3**   Sew the two vintage buttons for eyes to the face of the cat.

**4**   Stuff the base of the cat's body use dark stuffing.

**5**   Cut the feet off a pair of thick black tights (stockings) and place inside each other to make a double lining. Pour about 300 g (10½ oz) of aquarium pebbles into the feet and bind up tightly with a pencil in the centre of the weight.

**6**   Place the weight in the centre of the cat body and use more dark stuffing around the weight. Even out the stuffing all round and then fill the head, allowing the end of the pencil to come up to about halfway into the face of the cat.

**7**   Stuff all the way to the top and then using the long end of black yarn, stitch the top of the cat closed across the top.

**8**   Sew the cat tail on allowing the twisting and turning part of the tail to curl naturally around the base of the body of the cat.

**9**   Poke the pipe-cleaner whiskers through the cheeks of the cat and tweak for effect.

## NATALIE'S NOTES

When working in amigurumi it's easy to lose your place. Never panic. Try to make sense of where you are but don't spend hours trying to correct it. A small mistake in this cat will not be noticeable, so instead just carry on and try to establish a new point of reference.

# COUNTRY FLOWER CUSHION

A large summery cushion that features nine different sampler squares makes a strong statement piece. The back is made with rows of stripes reminiscent of deckchair ticking. The crisp, clear colours with hints of brights are perfect for summer.

## MATERIALS

**Yarn**: Sirdar Baby Bamboo DK, 50 g (1¾ oz)

- 3 x Cream, col no 131 (Cream)
- 2 x Rinky dink pink, col no 158 (Bright pink)
- 2 x Perky pink, col no 124 (Light pink)
- 2 x Yellow submarine, col no 157 (Yellow)
- 2 x Limey, col no 155 (Green)
- 1 x Jelly baby, col no 153 (Orange)
- 1 x Scooter, col no 149 (Blue)
- 1 x Babe, col no 134 (Pale lilac)
- 1 x Flip flop, col no 125 (Dark lilac)

Wool sewing needle

Scissors

1 cushion insert 46 cm (18 in) square

**Hook**: 3 mm

## TENSION

Using a 3 mm hook each square measures 15 cm (6 in) with 14 stitches and 10 rows.

## FINISHED SIZE

46 cm (18 in) square

## PATTERN

Each square is made using double crochet with a base of 25 foundation chain and 32 rows of dc. The squares are stitched together to make a large square. The back of the cushion is made in rows of dc

## BASIC PATTERN FOR SQUARES

Ch 25.

**Row 1**: In second ch from hk, make 1 dc and into each chain across. Turn. (Beg ch counts as first dc in this and every row.) Turn [25dc].

**Row 2**: Ch 1; dc into each dc across. Turn [25dc].

Repeat row 2 another 30 times. Fasten off leaving a long tail for sewing [32 rows in total].

## CUSHION ASSEMBLY DIAGRAM

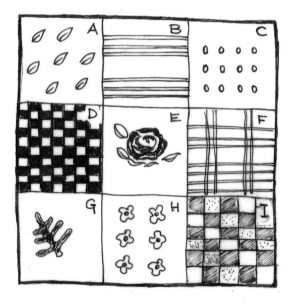

## LITTLE LEAVES SQUARE (A)

Make a square in green following the Basic Pattern.

Make 3 orange, 3 yellow and 2 dark lilac leaves.

Ch 5.

**Row 1**: Into second ch from hk make 1 dc; 1 htr into next ch; 1 tr into next ch; 3 dc into last ch, turning work as you go. Into the unused ch lps from beg 5ch, work as follows: 1 htr into each of the next 2 lps; 1 dc into each of the next 2 lps. Join with a sl st to the first dc made. Fasten off. Leave a tail long enough to sew leaf to the cushion as indicated in the drawing.

## TICKING SQUARE (B)

Begin as for Basic Pattern using blue and change colours as follows: (see Techniques for changing colour).

4 rows blue.

2 rows yellow.

1 row bright pink.

3 rows orange.

1 row cream.

10 rows blue.

1 row cream.

3 rows orange.

1 row bright pink.

2 rows yellow.

4 rows blue.

Fasten off and leave a long tail for sewing up.

 Country Flower Cushion

## PINEAPPLE BOBBLE SQUARE (C)

**Pineapple st**: *Yo, insert hk into specified place, yo and pull through, yo and pull through 2 lps on hk; rep from * 5 times, yo and pull through all 7 lps on hk.

With cream begin Basic Pattern for rows 1–10.

**Row 11**: Ch 1; 1 dc in each of next 5 dc; change colour to bright pink, and keeping the cream yarn under the pineapple, make a pineapple st directly below the next st into row 9. **Change colour to cream, and keeping the pineapple yarn colour on the side of the work facing you make 1 dc into each of the next 4 dc; make pineapple st in bright pink as before. Rep from ** twice more; 1 dc into each of next 6 dc. Turn.

**Rows 12–16**: Work as for row 2 of Basic Pattern.

**Row 17**: Repeat row 11, changing to lilac for each pineapple and working into row 15 below.

**Rows 18–22**: Work as for row 2 of Basic Pattern.

**Row 23**: Repeat row 11, changing to blue for each pineapple and working into row 21 below.

**Row 25–32**: Work as for row 2 of Basic Pattern. Fasten off leaving a long tail for sewing.

## GINGHAM SQUARE (D)

Begin as for Basic Pattern in dark lilac, and change to cream for the gingham checks following the chart below. The chart shows the first 10 rows. Repeat the pattern from rows 3–10, five times. Fasten off and leave a long tail for sewing.

## ROSE CENTRE (E)

In cream, begin as for Basic Pattern for rows 1–7 and then work the chart on the following page, changing colours as appropriate. Cream, light pink, bright pink

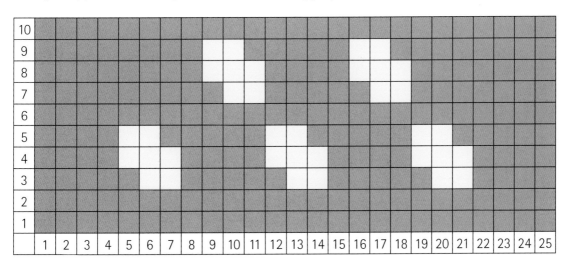

and green are used. Work rows 27–32 in cream.

## PINK CHECKED SQUARE (F)

Begin in bright pink as for Basic Pattern and continue as follows:

3 rows bright pink.
1 row cream.
5 rows bright pink.
1 row cream.
2 rows bright pink.
1 row cream.
1 row bright pink.

1 row cream.
7 rows bright pink.
1 row cream.
2 rows bright pink.
1 row cream.
3 rows bright pink.
1 row cream.
2 rows bright pink.

Fasten off leaving a long tail for sewing. With cream, top stitch at right angles starting at the bottom of the square and 7 sts in from the left. Work another row of top stitching

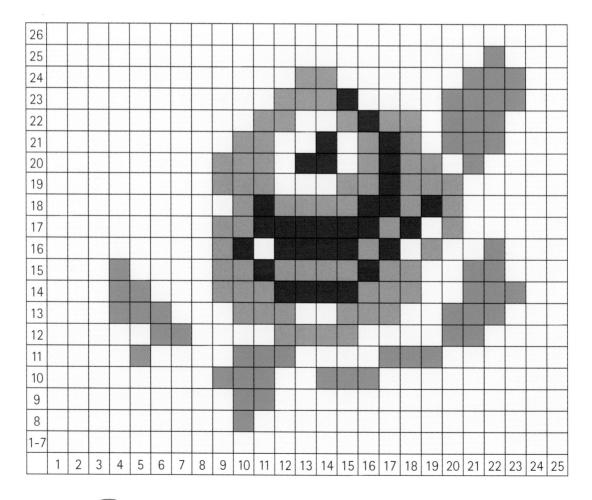

Country Flower Cushion

into the ninth st from the left. Repeat the two rows of stitching on the right-hand side of the square. Weave in these ends.

See Techniques for Top Stitching.

## FERN LEAF SQUARE (G)
Make a square in yellow following the Basic Pattern.

### Fern Leaf Pattern
A centre line of chains forms the foundation. Each side part of the leaf is created using ch sts, dc and htr.

In green, ch 15.

**Row 1**: (1 dc, 1 htr) into second ch from hk; 1 dc into each of next 3 ch; ch 6; (1 dc, 1 htr) into second ch from hk; 1 dc into each of next 4 ch; and returning to beg 15ch, 1 dc into each of the next 3 ch; ch 7; (1 dc, 1 htr) into second ch from hk; 1 htr into next ch; (1 htr, 1 dc) into next ch; 1 dc into each of next 3 ch; and returning to beg 15ch, 1 dc into each of the next 3 ch; ch 8; (1 dc, 1 htr) into second ch from hk; 1 htr in next ch; 2 htr into next ch; 1 dc into each of next 4 ch; and returning to beg 15ch, 1 dc into each of next 2 ch; 3 dc into last ch. Rotate work and using the unused lps on the other side of the beg 15ch, work as follows: 1 dc into next lp; ch 7; (1 dc, 1 htr) into second ch from hk; 1 htr into ch; 1 dc into each of next 4 ch; and returning to beg 15ch, 1 dc into each of the next 4 lps; ch 6; (1 dc, 1 htr) into second ch from hk; 1 htr into next ch; 1 dc into each of next 3 ch;

and returning to beg 15ch, 1 dc into each of next 5 lps; ch 5 (1 dc, 1 htr) into second ch from hk; 1 dc into each of next 3 ch; and returning to beg 15ch, 1 dc into each of the next 3 lps; 1 dc into first ch; join with sl st to first dc made. Fasten off leaving a long tail with which to sew the leaf to the square.

Position the leaf on the square so that it is at an angle. Sew to background square just inside the edges of the fern leaf. Weave in ends.

## FORGET-ME-NOTS (H)
Make a square in pale lilac following the Basic Pattern.

### Flowers
Make 6. With yellow, ch 2.

**Row 1**: Into second ch from hk make 8 dc. (Ensure that you are working into the bottom lp of the chain to prevent the st slipping.) Join with sl st to second dc, and change colour to blue on sl st.

**Row 2**: Ch 2; 3 tr into same st as joining; sl st into next dc; (4 tr into next dc, sl st into next dc) three times. Join with sl st to first ch of beg 2ch. Fasten off.

Weave in blue ends.

Position the flowers using the drawing as a guide and attach to the square by stitching through the yellow centres. Weave in all ends.

## DIAGONAL CHECK SQUARE (I)

Using green, orange, cream, yellow, blue and light pink make the square as follows:
Begin as for Basic Pattern in green.

**Rows 2—6**: In green, 1 dc into each of the next 5 dc; changing colour to cream, 1 dc in each of the next 5 dc; changing colour to green, 1 dc in each of the next 5 dc; changing colour to orange, 1 dc in each of the next 5 dc; changing colour to green, 1 dc in each of the next 5 dc. Turn.

**Rows 7—31**: Follow the same principle following the chart below for colour changes. Each square represents 5 sts and 5 rows.

**Row 32**: In green, 1 dc into each st across. Fasten off leaving a long tail for sewing.

## CUSHION BACK

Ch 75.

**Row 1**: In bright pink, in second ch from hk, make 1 dc and into each ch across. (Beg ch counts as first dc in this and every row.) Turn [75dc].

**Row 2**: Ch 1, dc into each dc across. Turn [75dc].

Repeat row 2 another 93 times making the colour changes as indicated below.

6 rows bright pink.

3 rows cream.

7 rows green.

2 rows cream.

4 rows orange.

2 rows blue.

5 rows orange.

2 rows cream.

7 rows green.

3 rows cream.

13 rows light pink.

3 rows cream.

7 rows orange.

2 rows cream.

5 rows yellow.

2 rows blue.

4 rows yellow.

2 rows cream.

7 rows green.

3 rows cream.

6 rows bright pink.

Fasten off (total rows 95).

## MAKING UP

Weave in all ends on the back panel. Sew the squares to each other following the Cushion Assembly Diagram. Weave in all colour change ends on all the squares. Sew the front to the back with right sides facing until you have completed three sides. Turn right side out and insert the cushion pad. Sew opening closed.

## EDGING

Cut 12 strands of cream yarn, each measuring 3 times the circumference of the cushion: 550 cm (216 in). Split the yarn into 3 bunches of 4 strands each and plait together. Begin attaching the plait as you work around the cushion. Sew the centre of the plait to the sides of the cushion, using cream thread, checking to make sure the plait neatly covers the join.

## BLOCKING

It should not be necessary to block this cushion using the materials specified. However, if different yarns are used and they have a tendency to curl, then it is better to steam block the item.

## VARIATION

It is possible to make a smaller cushion using fewer squares or even to make a quilt or a baby quilt from this pattern by repeating and increasing the number of sampler squares.

## NATALIE'S NOTES

As this cushion is not lined, it is important to choose a good quality feather insert with a strong cover, or else make a separate lining in order to prevent errant feathers creeping out of the cushion.

# GRACE FLOWER NAPKIN RING

Inspired by 1950s jewellery, this simple but beautifully shaped flower is sculpted in crochet and used to embellish a napkin ring.

## MATERIALS
**Yarn**: Rowan Cotton Glace, 50 g (1¾ oz)
- Persimmon, col no 832 (Orange)
- Green Slate, col no 844 (Green)
- Poppy, col no 741 (Red)

Wool sewing needle

Scissors

**Hook**: 2.5 mm

## TENSION
Tension is not important for this pattern.

## FINISHED SIZE
The flower measures 12 cm (4½ in) in diameter. The ring is 4.5 cm (2 in) wide and 14 cm (5 ½in) long before it is joined into a circle.

## SPECIAL PATTERN STITCHES

**Begvst = Beginning Treble V-stitch**: Work
1 tr into next st, leaving last lp on k, sk 1 st,
into next ch work 1 tr leaving last lp on hk,
yo and draw through all 3 lps on hk.

**Vst = Treble V stitch**: Work 1 tr into first
ch sp leaving last lp on hk; into next ch sp
work 1 tr leaving last lp on hk, yo and draw
through all 3 lps on hk. The first part of the
next vst is worked into the same ch sp as
the second part of the previous vst.

## PATTERN

Each petal is made separately.

## FLOWER CENTRE

In red, ch 2.

**Row 1**: 8 dc into second ch (using bottom
lp) [8dc].

**Row 2**: 2 dc into each [16dc]. Fasten off. Do
not weave in ends.

## FLOWER

In orange, ch 14.

**Row 1**: 1 dc into second ch from hk; 1 dc
into each of the next 2 ch; 1 htr into each of
next 2 ch; 2 tr into next ch; 1 dtr into each
of next 2 ch;1 tr into next ch; 1 htr into each
of next 2 ch; 1 dc into next ch; 3 dc into last
ch; (and rotating work, continue working
using the unused lps from the beg 14ch);

1 dc into next lp; 1 htr into each of the next
3 lps; 1 tr into next lp; 2 tr into next lp;
1 dtr into next lp; 2 tr into next lp; 1 htr into
each of next 3 lps; 1 dc in last lp and sl st to
last lp. (This end is the centre of the petal.)

## BAND

In green, ch 26.

**Row 1**: 1 htr into third ch from hk, (first
2 ch counts as a htr here and throughout);
1 htr into each ch across. Turn [25htr].

**Row 2**: Ch 3 (counts as a tr here and
throughout); 1 tr into next htr; ch 1;
(1 beg vst, ch 2) 6 times; 1 beg vst; ch 1; 1 tr
into each of next 2 ch. Turn [7 beg vst].

**Row 3**: Ch 3; 1 tr into next tr, ch 1; (1 vst,

ch 2) 6 times; 1 vst; ch 1; 1 tr into each of next 2 tr. Turn [7vst].

**Row 4**: Ch 3; 1 tr in next tr; 1 tr in 1ch sp; (1 tr in top of vst, 2 tr into 2ch sp) 6 times; 1 tr into top of vst; 1 tr in 1ch sp; 1 tr into each of next 2 tr. Turn [25tr].

**Row 5**: Ch 2; 1 htr in each tr across. Fasten off, leaving a long tail for sewing [25htr].

## MAKING UP

Place 2 petals alongside each other and right side up. Sew together under the Vs from the centre point through the first 8 sts. Place the red centre wrong side up in the middle of the petals and sew in place.

Sew the band together along the narrow edge and attach the flower so it covers the join. If you are making a number of napkin rings make sure that you position all the flowers in a similar way.

## BLOCKING

It is not necessary to block this project, but it can be starched, see Techniques.

## VARIATION

This flower could be used to embellish any manner of things such as curtain tiebacks or guest hand towels. The flower could be made to attach to a hairpiece and its sculptural effect can be heightened by using a smaller hook size to make the stitches tighter and the shaping more intense.

# cache POTS

These dinky little pots are perfect for holding precious bits and pieces. Because they are easy to make they make perfect gifts. Have fun embellishing them.

**MATERIALS**

**Yarn**: Patons Linen Touch DK, 50 g (1¾ oz)
- Cherry, col no 030 (Red)
- Mandarin, col no 026 (Yellow)
- Aqua, col no 065 (Blue)

Wool sewing needle

Scissors

Assorted buttons and beads

**Hook**: 2.5 mm

**TENSION**

The tighter the tension the better the pots will stand. 9 stitches and 10 rows = 5 cm (2 in) square.

**FINISHED SIZE**

Large cache pot has a diameter of 12.5 cm (5 in) and is 10.5 cm (4 in) tall.

Medium cache pot has a diameter of 8 cm (3¼ in) and is 9 cm (3½ in) tall.

Small cache pot has a diameter of 7.5 cm (3 in) and is 45 cm (2 in) tall.

## PATTERN

This is an amigurumi type of pattern and starts from the centre in a spiral and the rows are not joined. Each Cache Pot is worked with a flattened base, straight sides and a turned back edge. The wrong side of the pots are meant to be visible as this has an attractive texture.

## LARGE CACHE POT

In red, ch 2.

**Row 1**: 8 dc into second ch from hk. Do not join.

**Row 2**: 2 dc into each dc [16dc]. (Place a stitch marker in last dc in this row and move the marker to the last st of each row as you work.)

**Row 3**: *1 dc into next dc, 2 dc into next dc. Repeat from * round [24dc].

**Row 4**: *1 dc into each of the next 2 dc; 2 dc into next dc. Repeat from * round [32dc].

**Row 5**: *1 dc into each of the next 3 dc; 2 dc into next dc. Repeat from * round [40dc].

**Row 6**: *1 dc into each of the next 4 dc; 2 dc into next dc. Repeat from * round [48dc].

**Row 7**: *1 dc into each of the next 5 dc; 2 dc into next dc. Repeat from * round [56dc].

**Row 8**: *1 dc into each of the next 6 dc; 2 dc into next dc. Repeat from * round [64dc].

**Row 9**: 1 dc into back lp of each dc. (This forms a ridge and gives the pot some definition.)

**Rows 10–26**: 1 dc into each dc.

**Row 27**: *1 dc into each of the next 7 dc; 2 dc into next dc. Repeat from * round [72dc].

**Rows 28–34**: 1 dc into each dc [72dc]. Sl st into next dc.

Fasten off and weave in ends.

## MEDIUM CACHE POT

In orange, complete as for the Large Cache Pot pattern up to and including row 6 and continue as follows:

**Row 7**: 1 dc into back lp of each dc [48dc].
**Rows 8–16**: 1 dc into each dc [48dc].
**Row 17**: * 1 dc into each of the next 5 dc, 2 dc into next dc. Repeat from * round [56dc].
**Rows 18–20**: 1 dc into each dc [56dc]. Sl st into next dc.
Fasten off and weave in ends.

## SMALL CACHE POT

In blue, complete as for the Large Cache Pot pattern up to and including row 5 and continue as follows:
**Row 6**: 1 dc into back lp of each dc [40dc].
**Rows 7–14**: 1 dc into each dc [40dc].
**Row 15**: *1 dc into each of the next 4 dc; 2 dc into next dc. Repeat from * round [48dc].
**Rows 16–18**: 1 dc into each dc [48dc]. Sl st into next dc.
Fasten off and weave in ends.

## FINISHING AND EMBELLISHING

Turn down the flap at the point where the last set of increased stitches was made. The main body of the pot should be inside out, while the turned back flap will be right side out.

For the large red pot, 4 vintage buttons were used for decoration. On the medium orange pot assorted glass beads were stitched on around the edge, while on the small blue pot, cream seed beads were slip-stitched around the edge and dotted closely all around the turned back flap.

## BLOCKING

It is not necessary to block this project but if you want to stiffen the pot, use the starching method described in Techniques.

## VARIATION

The pattern can be used with various materials to create pots for all purposes, just vary the hook size to match the material. Try experimenting with alternatives such as string, jute or raffia.

## NATALIE'S NOTES

I love rummaging around charity shops and car boot sales for buttons and beads. Often bead necklaces are sold for very little cost and yield a large number of beads. Find ways to store your beads and buttons so that they are easily accessible when you want to be creative.

# aQUaRIUS FLOORMaT

A casual modern country-style floormat that is very easy to make. It is made in the most basic and classic granny square pattern, and is felted to create a chunky check which is sewn with a contrasting thread to give it an ethnic feel.

**MATERIALS**

**Yarn**: Rico Creative Flitz, 50 g (1¾ oz)
- 6 x col no 70 (Yellow)
- 6 x col no 19 (Pink)
- 6 x col no 36 (Blue)

Large wool sewing needle

Scissors

**Hook**: 10 mm

**TENSION**

**Tension** is not important for this pattern. The tighter you work the smaller the finished squares are and the denser the finished piece.

**FINISHED SIZE**

76 x 152 cm (30 x 60 in) before felting.

60 x 111 cm (24 x 44 in) after felting.

**Note** There is just sufficient yarn to make the floormat. It's not necessary to leave very long ends as the felting process will secure the wool. Work over your beginning tail end in the first row and try not to waste yarn. If your mat does not shrink by at least a third after washing, then repeat the felting process.

## PATTERN

This pattern is made up of 45 motifs that are sewn together, in the order shown below in the Colour Layout Diagram. Make 15 in each colour.

**Row 1**: Ch 4 (counts as a tr and a 2ch sp); (3 tr, ch 2) 3 times; 2 tr. Join with sl st to second ch of beg 4ch.

## COLOUR LAYOUT DIAGRAM

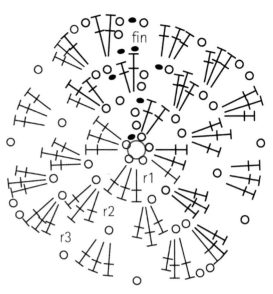

**Row 2**: Sl st into 2ch sp, ch 2, 2 tr, ch 2, 3 tr, (beg corner); ch 1; (in next 2ch sp work (3 tr, 2 ch, 3 tr) (corner made); ch 1) 3 times. Join with sl st to second ch of beg 2ch.

**Row 3**: Sl st into each tr; into 2ch sp, work beg corner; ch 1; (in next 1ch sp work 3 tr; ch 1; in next 2ch sp work corner; ch 1) 3 times; 3 tr in next 1ch sp, ch 1. Join with sl st to second ch of beg 2ch. Fasten off.

## MAKING UP

Sew the motifs side by side and stitch under the double Vs of each stitch. Use one doubled length of acrylic for each seam across the entire length of each row and across the width of the mat. When reaching the corners make a backstitch under the V loops to tighten the join where the motifs meet.

Once all seams are sewn, pull the acrylic sewing threads tight so that the squares pucker a little. The whole rug will shrink once felted but there is a tendency for the corners to pull away. Knot the ends of the acrylic threads.

After felting sew any gaps that may have appeared. Tie the ends of the acrylic sewing yarn again and trim to about 4 cm (1½ in) to give a tassel effect.

## VARIATION

You can make larger or smaller mats by making more or less motifs. Since this is a classic granny square pattern you can also make each motif larger by continuing from row 3. The corners are always made in the 2ch sps, while 3 trs are made in the 1ch sp. After felting small holes appear between the bunches of trebles and make a bubble effect, which is different and fun.

## NATALIE'S NOTES

Plain and straightforward, the granny square has been used for many years and is often seen in vintage blankets framed in black yarn.

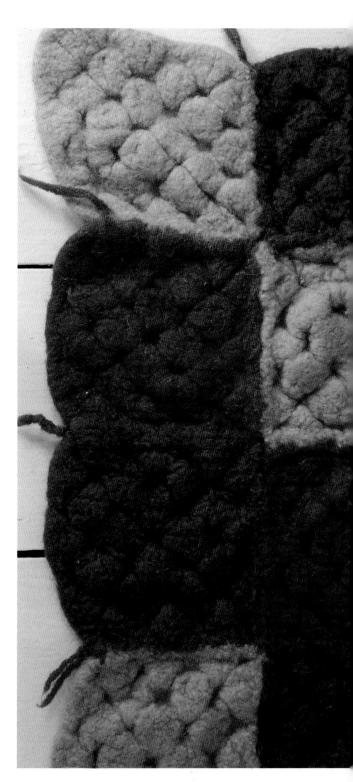

# POPPY BAG

A contemporary and stylish accessory for the bathroom, this pretty bag can be lined with plastic making it ideal for storing your make up and trinkets. It is embellished with a large poppy sculpted in crochet.

**MATERIALS**
**Yarn**: Rowan Hand Knit Cotton DK, 50 g (1¾ oz)
- 3 x Mist, col no 341 (White)
Rowan Cotton Glace, 50 g (1¾ oz)
- 1 x Poppy, col no 741 (Red)
- 1 x Black, col no 727 (Black)
- Small amount Ivy, col no 812 (Yellow/green)
Wool sewing needle
Scissors
Cardboard for base
50 cm (20 in) lining—either fabric or waterproof material
**Hooks**: 4 mm and 2.5 mm
**TENSION**
A 10 cm (4 in) square is made up of 14 stitches and 12 rows.
**FINISHED SIZE**
25 x 20 cm (10 x 8 in).

## SPECIAL PATTERN STITCH

**Htr2tog = Half treble decrease**: Yo, insert hk into next st, yo, pull through, yo, insert hk into following st, yo, pull through, yo and pull through all 5 lps on hk (decrease made).

## PATTERN

The bag is worked in a spiral in a similar way to the Black Cat Doorstop using a half treble stitch (htr). The bag is made from the base upwards and the rows are not joined. The wrong side of the work will be shown. In white, ch 26 loosely.

Follow the pattern instructions for the Black Cat Doorstop from the Foundation Row to the end of row 3. Use a 4 mm hook.

**Rows 4–12**: Repeat row 3 [78htr].

**Row 13**: (1 htr into next 19 htr, htr2tog, 1 htr into next 16 htr, htr2tog) twice [74htr].

**Row 14**: 1 htr into next 20 htr; htr2tog; 1 htr into next 12 htr; htr2tog; 1 htr into next 21 htr; htr2tog; 1 htr into next 13 htr; htr2tog [70htr].

**Row 15**: 1 htr in each htr [70htr].

**Rows 16–19**: Repeat row 15.

**Row 20**: (Ch 26; sk 26 htr; 1 htr into next 9 htr) twice (to form the handles).

**Row 21**: (1 htr into each of 26 ch and into next 9 htr) twice [70htr].

**Row 22**: 1 htr into each of the next 68 sts;

1 dc into next st and sl st into last st. Fasten off.

## POPPY

For each part start with a long tail of yarn to use for sewing later. The 2ch at the beg of each row counts as an htr. Use a 2.5 mm hook for all parts of the poppy.

### Small Petal

Make 2.

**Row 1**: Ch 3; 2 htr into third ch from hk. Turn [3htr].

**Row 2**: Ch 2; 2 htr into next htr; 2 htr into last htr. Turn [5htr].

**Row 3**: Ch 2; 3 htr into next htr; 2 htr into next htr; 3 htr into next htr; 1 htr into last htr. Turn [10htr].

**Row 4**: Ch 2; 3 htr into next htr; (2 htr into next htr) 6 times; 3 htr into next htr; 1 htr into last htr. Turn [20htr].

**Row 5**: Ch 2; (3 htr into next htr) 9 times; 1 htr into next 2 htr. Fasten off. Leave a long tail for sewing. Do not weave in ends [30htr].

### Large Petal

Make 2.

**Row 1**: Ch 5; 3 htr into third ch from hk; 1 htr into next ch; 3 htr into last ch. Turn [8htr].

**Row 2**: Ch 2; (2 htr into next htr) 6 times; 1 htr into last htr. Turn [14htr].

**Row 3**: Ch 2; 3 htr into next htr; (2 htr into next htr) 10 times; 3 htr into next htr; 1 htr into last htr. Turn [28htr].

**Row 4**: Ch 2; 1 htr into each across. Turn [28htr].

**Row 5**: Ch 2; 2 htr into next htr; (1 htr into next htr, 3 htr into next htr, 1 htr into next htr) twice; 5 htr into next htr; *1 htr into next htr; 2 htr into next htr; 1 htr into next htr; 5 htr into next htr; ** 1 htr into each of next 2 htr; 5 htr into next htr. Repeat from * to **. [43htr]. Fasten off. Leave a long tail for sewing. Do not weave in ends

## Black Centre

Ch 5 and join with sl st to form a ring.
**Row 1**: (Ch 5, dc into ring.) Rep 12 times [12dc]. Fasten off. Leave a long tail for sewing. Do not weave in ends.

## ASSEMBLY

Pleat the base of each petal by bringing the bottom edge to the bottom centre. Place the smaller petals over the larger petals at 90 degrees. Pin in place. Pin black centre in the middle and sew all three layers together using the tail ends. In a couple of places slip stitch the smaller petals to the larger ones so that the poppy petals stay upright.

Taking a small amount of green/yellow yarn cut five lengths about 7 cm (3 in) long and knot tightly together about 2 cm (3/4 in) from the end. Thread the long ends through the centre of the poppy to form stamens and pull through. Trim ends of the stamen. Weave in all other ends and sew poppy to bag.

## LINING THE BAG

1    From lining, cut two pieces for the sides about 55 x 17 cm (21 x 6 in) and test fit.

2    Cut the base from cardboard 25 x 12 cm (10 x 5 in). Test fit and adjust as necessary. Trim the edges of the card so they are rounded.

3    Cut two pieces of lining 1 cm larger than cardboard base. Stitch the lining sides together along the short edges. Flatten seam.

4    Pin to both pieces of base without the cardboard. Stitch all around, inserting cardboard when you have almost completed the sewing. Sew gap closed.

5    Place the lining inside the bag with the seams facing the interior of the bag. Turn the top edge under and pin the top of the lining to the inside of the bag ensuring that you have a fit with some ease. Using a hemstitch, sew the lining to the top of the bag.

## VARIATION

The poppy is a useful embellishment for all sorts of projects including clothing and hats. The poppy can be made in other materials to decorate a handbag or even an evening bag.

Poppy Bag

# Bead Door Curtain

Light and breezy and full of fun this retro-look bead curtain is straight out of 1970s folklore.

## MATERIALS

**Yarn**: Stylecraft Special DK, 100g (3½ oz) Only small amounts of the following colours are used:

- Aspen, col no 1422 (Sea green)
- Bright green, col no 1259 (Neon green)
- Citron, col no 1263 (Pale yellow)
- Clematis, col no 1390 (Pale lilac)
- Fiesta, col no 1257 (Bright pink)
- Fondant pink, col no 1241 (Pink)
- Jaffa, col no 1256 (Bright Orange)
- Green, col no 1116 Green (Bright green)
- Lavender, col no 1188 (Lavender)
- Lipstick, col no 1246 (Bright red)
- Magenta, col no 1084 (Bright purple)
- Matador, col no 1010 (Deep red)
- Meadow, col no 1065 (Green)
- Sherbert, col no 1034 (Aqua)
- Shrimp, col no 1132 (Orange)
- Spring green, col no 1316 (Pale green)
- Sunshine, col no 1114 (Yellow)
- Turquoise, col no 1068 (Blue)
- Violet, col no 1277 (Purple)
- Walnut, col no 1054 (Brown)
- Wisteria, col no 1432 (Lilac)

For the strands use Aida crochet thread size 10 Col no 403 (Black)
Wool sewing needle
Scissors
Wood batten 1.5 cm (¾ in) square
2 mm and 6 mm drill bit
3 brass hooks
Synthetic stuffing
Quick-setting fabric adhesive
3 small closed screw-in hooks
**Hooks**: 3.5 mm, 3 mm and 1.75 mm

## TENSION

Is not important for this pattern.

## FINISHED SIZE

Each strand is 220 cm (86 in) long, but tailor it to fit your doorway. Do not allow the beads to drag on the floor.

## SPECIAL PATTERN STITCH

**Dc2tog = Double crochet decrease** Insert hk into specified st, yo and draw through, insert hk into next st, yo and draw through, yo and draw through all 3 lps on hk (decrease made).

## PATTERN

There are several different types of beads here, so make as many of each as you want and in any colour combinations you like. Read the Assembly instructions before you decide how many beads to make. Make up the batten first so you can assemble the design as you make the parts.

## FLOWER BEADS

Ch 4. Join with sl st to form a ring.
**Row 1**: Ch 2 (counts as an htr here and throughout); 11 htrs into ring. Join with sl st to second ch of beg 2ch. Fasten off [12htr].
**Row 2**: In second colour, join into any st, ch 2; (1 tr, ch 1, 2 tr) into same st; (sl st into next htr; (2 tr, ch 1, 2 tr) into next htr) 5 times; sl st into next htr. Join with sl st to the back of the first ch from beg 2ch. Fasten off. Weave in the ends.
Placing wrong sides together sew the centres of the 2 beads tog. Using the tail ends of the first colour used, stitch the two beads together round the Vs of row 1. Do not sew

together the petals formed in row 2. Tuck any loose ends inside the centres to give a little bit of stuffing.

## TRIPLE YO-YOS

In any colour; ch 4. Join with sl st to form a ring.
**Row 1**: Ch 1; 12 dc into ring. Join with sl st to first dc.
**Row 2**: Ch 2 (counts as an htr here); 1 htr into same st; 2 htr into each dc around. Join with sl st to second ch of beg 2ch [24htr]. Take 3 yoyos – use different colours – and place them on top of each other like a sandwich. Stitch together firmly passing the needle through the dc row from top to bottom of the stack. Only a few stitches are required. Weave in all other ends.

## MINI HYPERBOLICS

In any colour, ch 2.
**Row 1**: Into second ch from hk make 12 dc. Join with sl st to first dc [12dc].
**Row 2**: Ch 3; 3 tr into same dc as joining; 4 tr into each dc around. Join with sl st to third ch of beg 3ch. Fasten off [48tr].
**Optional**: Add a row of another colour to the edge of the hyberbolic, if you like, by making a row of dcs along the edge [48dc].

## LARGE BEAD

In any colour, ch 2.
**Row 1**: Into second ch from hk make 12 dc. Join with sl st to first dc [12 dc].
**Row 2**: Ch 1, 1 dc into same sp as joining; 1

dc into next dc; (2 dc into next dc, 1 dc into each of next 3 dc) twice; 2 dc into next dc; 1 dc into last dc. Join with sl st to first dc [15dc].

**Row 3**: Ch 1, 1 dc into same sp as joining; 1 dc into each of next 2 dc; (2 dc into next dc; 1 dc into each of next 4 dc) twice; 2 dc into next dc; 1 dc into last dc. Join with sl st to first dc [18dc].

**Row 4**: Ch 1, 1 dc into same sp as joining; 1 dc into each of next 3 dc; (2 dc into next dc, 1 dc into each of next 5 dc) twice; 2 dc into next dc; 1 dc into last dc. Join with sl st to first dc [21dc].

**Row 5**: Ch 1, 1 dc into each st around. Join with sl st to first dc [21dc].

**Row 6**: Ch 1, 1 dc into same sp as joining; 1 dc into each of next 3 dc; (dc2tog (decrease), 1 dc into each of next 5 dc) twice; dc2tog; 1 dc into last dc. Join with sl st to first dc [18dc].

**Row 7**: Ch 1, 1 dc into same sp as joining; 1 dc into each of next 2 dc; (dc2tog, 1 dc into each of next 4 dc) twice; dc2tog; 1 dc into last dc. Join with sl st to first dc [15dc].

**Row 8**: Ch 1, 1 dc into same sp as joining; 1 dc into next dc; (dc2tog, 1 dc into each of next 3 dc) twice; dc2tog; 1 dc into last dc. Join with sl st to first dc. Fasten off [12dc]. Stuff each ball generously but lightly. Sew the top closed by passing the needle through the sts and pulling gently to gather up. Weave in the ends.

## MEDIUM BEAD

In any colour, ch 2.

**Row 1**: Into second ch from hk make 9 dc. Join with sl st to first dc [9dc].

**Row 2**: Ch 1, 1 dc into same sp as joining; (2 dc into next dc, 1 dc into each of next 2 dc) twice; 2 dc into next dc; 1 dc into last dc. Join with sl st to first dc [12dc].

**Row 3**: Ch 1, 1 dc into same sp as joining; 1 dc into next dc, (2 dc into next dc, 1 dc into each of next 3 dc) twice; 2 dc into next dc; 1 dc into last dc. Join with sl st to first dc [15dc].

**Row 4**: Ch 1, 1 dc into each st around. Join with sl st to first dc [15dc].

**Row 5**: Ch 1, 1 dc into same sp as joining; 1 dc into next dc, (dc2tog, 1 dc into each of next 3 dc) twice; dc2tog; 1 dc into last dc. Join with sl st to first dc [12dc].

**Row 6**: Ch 1, 1 dc into same sp as joining; (dc2tog, 1 dc into each of next 2 dc) twice, dc2tog; 1 dc into last dc. Join with sl st to first dc. Fasten off [9dc].
Finish in the same way as for Large Bead.

## SMALL BEAD

In any colour, ch 2.

**Rows 1–2**: Work as for Medium Bead.

**Row 3**: Ch 1, 1 dc into each st around [12dc].

**Row 4**: Work as for row 6 of Medium Bead. Finish in the same way as for Large Bead.

*Bead Door Curtain*

## TINY BEAD

In any colour, ch 2.

**Row 1**: Into second ch from hk make 3 dc; do not join. Turn.

**Row 2**: Ch 1; 2 dc into each dc. Fasten off. There is no need to stuff these tiny beads; use the tail end to stitch through the 6 dc and pull the bead closed. Weave in ends, which will stuff the bead sufficiently.

## PEANUT BEAD

In any colour, ch 2.

**Row 1**: Into second ch from hk make 8 dc. Join with sl st to first dc [8dc].

**Row 2**: Ch 1, 1 dc into same sp as joining; 1 dc into next dc; (2 dc into next dc, 1 dc into next dc) three times; 2 dc into last dc. Join with sl st to first dc [12dc].

**Row 3**: Ch 1, 1 dc into each sp as joining; 1 dc into each st around. Join with sl st to first dc.

**Row 4**: Repeat row 3.

**Row 5**: Ch 1, 1 dc into same sp as joining; (dc2tog, 1 dc into next dc) three times, dc2tog. Join with sl st to first dc [8dc].

**Row 6**: Ch 1, 1 dc into each st around. Join with sl st to first dc [8dc].

**Row 7**: Repeat row 2 [12dc].

**Rows 8–9**: Repeat row 3 [12dc].

**Row 10**: Repeat row 5. Fasten off [8dc]. Finish as for Large Bead.

## TUBE BEAD

This is narrow cylinder. Row 1 provides the start, with row 2 worked only in the front lp, which allows a ridge to form at the top of the cylinder. Rows 2–11 (are worked straight but you can change colours and create your own interesting combinations. Row 11 is worked only in the front lp, so that you can begin to close off the tube.

In any colour, ch 2.

**Row 1**: Into second ch from hk make 12 dc. Join with sl st to first dc [12dc].

**Row 2**: Ch 1, working into front lp only; 1 dc into each st around. Join with sl st to first dc [12dc].

**Rows 3–10**: Ch 1, 1 dc into each st around. Join with sl st to first dc [12dc].

**Row 11**: Ch 1, working into front lp only; 1 dc into each st around. Join with sl st to first dc [12dc].

**Row 12**: Ch 1, 1 dc into each st around. Join with sl st to first dc. Fasten off [12dc]. Stuff as for other beads, closing the top of the bead with a series of gathering stitches. Weave in ends.

## HEART

In any colour, ch 2.

**Row 1**: 5 dc into second ch from hk. Join with sl st to first dc [5dc].

**Row 2**: Ch 1, 2 dc into same sp as joining; 2 dc into each of the next 4 dc. Join with sl st to first dc [10dc].
Fasten off. This is A.
With the same colour, start another heart (B) and follow the above two rounds, but do not fasten off.

**Row 3**: Insert hk into same sp as joining

and into any dc of A; sl st tog; insert hk into next dc of B and into next dc of A; sl st tog; continue working in B, 1 dc into each of next 8 dc; 1 dc into side of first sl st; 1 dc into each of the next 8 dc of A; 1 dc in side of second sl st. Join with a sl st to the first dc made [18dc].

**Row 4**: Ch 1, 1 dc into same sp as joining; 1 dc into each of next 2 dc; dc2tog; 1 dc into each of next 7 dc; dc2tog; 1 dc into each of next 4 dc. Join with sl st to first dc [16dc].

**Row 5**: Ch 1, 1 dc into same sp as joining; 1 dc into next dc; dc2tog; 1 dc into each of next 6 dc; dc2tog; 1 dc into each of next 4 dc. Join with sl st to first dc [14dc].

**Row 6**: Ch 1, 1 dc into same sp as joining; 1 dc into next dc; dc2tog; 1 dc into each of next 5 dc; dc2tog; 1 dc into each of next 3 dc. Join with sl st to first dc [12dc].

**Row 7**: Ch 1, 1 dc into same sp as joining; dc2tog; 1 dc into each of next 4 dc; dc2tog; 1 dc into each of next 3 dc. Join with sl st to first dc [10dc].

**Row 8**: Ch 1, 1 dc into same sp as joining; dc2tog; 1 dc into each of next 3 dc; dc2tog; 1 dc into each of next 2 dc [8dc]. Join with sl st to first dc. Stuff at the end of this round making sure that you fill the top halves of the heart well.

**Row 9**: Ch 1, 1 dc into same sp as joining; dc2tog; 1 dc into each of next 2 dc; dc2tog; 1 dc into next dc [6dc]. Join with sl st to first dc. Fasten off.

Pull the knot tight and weave in the ends so that the tip is pronounced. When threading onto the strands push through between the centre of the top mounds (A and B) and through the tip of the heart.

## STRANDS

In black crochet cotton and with a 1.75 mm hk, make a length of ch sts 20 cm (8 in) longer than the desired length.

## BATTEN COVER

With a 3.5 mm hk, make a foundation chain 5 cm (2 in) longer than the batten length.

**Row 1**: 1 dc into second ch from hk, 1 dc into each ch across, changing colour on the last st. Turn.

**Row 2**: Ch 1; 1 dc into each ch across, changing colour on the last st. Turn. Continue to repeat row 2 until you have made a strip wide enough to go all around the batten. Sew the long sides together over the batten. (Make the cover fairly tight but not so much that it stretches.

## POMPOMS

Make 6 pompoms each 4 cm (1½ in) in diameter in colours of your choice. See Techniques for instructions on how to make pompoms.

Bead Door Curtain

## ASSEMBLY

**1**  Measure the width of the doorway and add 10cm (4 in) extra. Cut a wood batten to the length of your measurement. (The batten I cut was 110 cm/43 in long).

**2**  An uneven number of strands looks better. Mark the centre of the batten, then measure and mark 5 cm (2 in) in from each end. Calculate how many strands will fit evenly on each side. The strands in the example photographed are set at 10 cm (4 in) intervals.

**3**  Double check your measurements, then drill the holes with a small drill bit—2 mm should be fine.

**4**  Countersink each hole with a 6 mm (1/4 in) drill bit to create a little hollow to allow the knot of the strands to disappear.

**5**  Cover the batten with the crocheted cover and tie off the ends. Crochet or plait the tail ends to give a relaxed funky tassel.

**6**  Attach the three pompoms to each side.

**7**  Screw 3 hooks evenly spaced to the top of the batten to hang the curtain above the door recess.

**8**  Thread the black strands through the holes and then knot firmly in place. Thread the bottom end onto a needle and begin to slide the beads up the strands to your chosen design.

**9**  Use the needle to pass through the bead from top to bottom. Once you are happy with the position of each, glue in place with a tiny about of fast-setting fabric glue.

**10**  Once the beads are in place, adjust the lengths of the strands to make them even at the bottom, ensuring the knot is big enough to prevent a bead slipping off.

## NATALIE'S NOTES

This project allows you to use colour imaginatively and the curtain would look great in almost every area, but especially near kitchens, conservatories, garden rooms and even tents. While the colours are bright, they are just tiny splashes and so will not overwhelm any colourscheme. Somehow a bead curtain has always seemed just a little bit decadent and naughty to me. Rebel a bit and have fun.

# UNION JaCK CUSHION

An iconic design worked in alternative colourways. This jacquard pattern has many colour changes, yet is made with a simple stitch.

**MATERIALS**

**Yarn**: Rowan Belle Organic DK 50 g (1¾ oz)
- 2 x Peony, col no 008 (Plum)
- 2 x Garnet, col no 021 (Pink)
- 1 x Moonflower, col no 013 (White)
- 1 x Clemantine, col no 020 (Orange)
- 1 x Ochre, col no 010 (Yellow)
- 1 x Grass, col no 019 (Green)
- 1 x Robins egg, col no 014 (Light blue)
- 1 x Cornflower, col no 002 (Dark blue)

Wool sewing needle
Scissors
Cushion pad: 33 x 43 cm (13 x 17 in)
3 buttons 1.5 cm (¾ in)
**Hook**: 4 mm

**TENSION**
Using a 4 mm hook a 10 cm (4 in) square uses 14 stitches and 11 rows.

**FINISHED SIZE**
33 x 43 cm (13 x 17 in)

## FRONT PATTERN

To change colour see Techniques.

Ch 57, loosely.

**Row 1**: 1 htr into third ch from hk, and into each ch across. Turn [56htr].

**Rows 2–36**: Ch 2; and following chart below make 1 htr into each htr across [56htr]. In row 2, for instance, ch 2 (counts as an htr here and throughout), 1 htr in next htr, changing colour to white on the last part of the htr; 1 htr into each of the next htr, changing colour to plum on the second st; 1 htr into the next 17 htrs, changing colour to white; and so on.

Fasten off at the end of the last round.

## BACK

The back is made in two parts that button together. The button opening allows a cushion pad to be inserted. The back consists of 3 rows in each colour as follows:

## COLOUR CHART

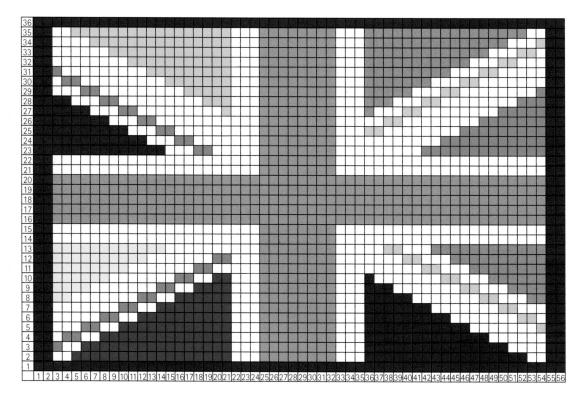

When working this chart—work from the bottom up. Row 1 is from left to right and row two is right to left.

  Union Jack Cushion

## Top Part

In plum, ch 55. (The back is made slightly smaller than the front.)

**Rows 1–3**: Ch 2; 1 htr into each of the htr [54htr].

**Rows 4–6**: Ch 2; 1 htr in next htr. Change to yellow and repeat row 1, making the last 2 htr in plum. Turn.

**Row 7**: Ch 2; 1 htr in next htr. Change to dark blue and repeat row 1, making the last 2 htr in plum. Turn.

**Row 8**: Ch 2; 1 htr in next htr; change to dark blue; 1 htr into next 4 htr; (ch 2; 1 htr into next 18 htr) twice; ch 2; 1 htr into next 4 htr, change to plum; 1 htr into each of next 2 htr. Turn (buttonholes made).

**Row 9**: Ch 2; 1 htr into next htr, change to dark blue; 1 htr into each htr and into each ch of the 2ch sts; ending the row with the last 2 htr being in plum. Turn [54htr].

**Row 10**: Ch 2; 1 htr into next htr, change to pink; and repeat row 1, making the last 2 htr in plum. Fasten off.

## Bottom Part

Working from the bottom up.

**Row 1**: In plum; 1 htr into third ch from hk, and into each ch across. Turn [54htr].

**Rows 2–3**: Ch 2; 1 htr into each htr across. Turn [54htr].

**Rows 4–6**: Ch 2; 1 htr into next htr. Change to green and continue as for row 2, ending the row with the last 2 htr being in plum. Turn.

Continue three rows of each colour in the following order: dark blue, pink, yellow, light blue, orange, green, pink. Make 2 rows in dark blue. Fasten off [29 rows in total].

## MAKING UP

Sew the buttons in place on the larger of the two pieces for the back.

Arrange the front over the back with wrong sides together. With the purple, dc through both layers beginning in any corner and working (2 dc, ch 1) into each of the corners. Dc into beginning dc, and fasten off.

## VARIATION

This pattern could be made in the traditional colours of red, white and blue. You could use the design for all manner of Union Jack related items.

## NATALIE'S NOTES

The Union Jack is not a symmetrical pattern, the bottom corners are the reverse of the top opposite corners. Purists will point out that this flag is upside down. Popular culture in the 1960s saw the motif used as clothing and even on the mini car.

Union Jack Cushion

# HOT HEART COSY

An extravagant pure wool cover for your hot water bottle is perfect for cuddling on a cold winter's night. This is a relaxed and simple design with a large heart on one side. It is finished with a chunky ribbed collar. The yarn is a speciality indie hand-dyed yarn with gentle waves of colour.

## MATERIALS
**Yarn**: Colourspun Pure Merino DK, 50 g (1³/₄ oz)
- 2 x col no 12 (Turquoise)
- 1 x col no 5 (Red)

Wool sewing needle
Scissors
Hot water bottle, 2 litre (70 fl oz)
**Hook**: 4.5 mm

## TENSION
Using a 4.5 mm hook, a 10 cm (4 in) square, using the main pattern stitch, uses 14 stitches across and 10 rows.

## FINISHED SIZE
33 x 22 cm (13 x 8½ in) including cuff. The width of the cosy is 22 cm (8½ in)

## SPECIAL PATTERN STITCH

**Rdcr = Raised double crochet rib**

This stitch is formed over two rows and creates a raised rib useful for collars, cuffs and caps. The foundation row st requires that dcs are made using only the back lp of the previous row. The front lp will be at the back of the work once it is turned and will stand out once the following row is made.

Insert hk into back lp of dc made in previous row and into the unused lp from row 2, yo and pull through both lps, yo and pull through to make dc. Continue as required by the pattern.

## PATTERN

Ch 2 at beginning of each row counts as a htr throughout this pattern.

## BACK

In turquoise, ch 29.

**Row 1**: 1 htr into third ch from hk, and into each ch across. Turn [28 htr].

**Row 2**: Ch 2; 1 htr into each htr across. Turn [28htr].

**Rows 3–28**: Repeat row 2. Fasten off.

## FRONT

See Techniques for how to change colour.
See chart below for heart design.
Begin as for back and work 8 rows of htr as for back with turquoise.

**Row 9**: 1 htr into first 13 htr, changing to red on the 13th st. Make 1 htr into each of

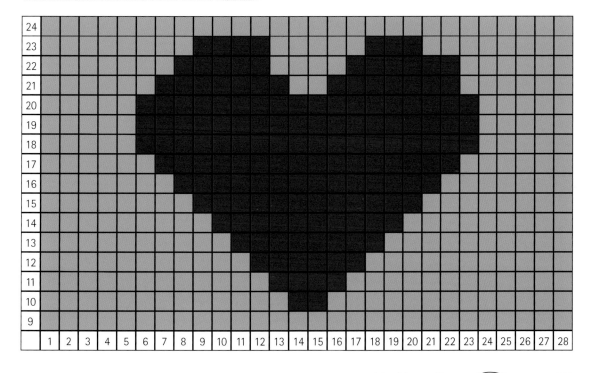

next 2 htr, changing colour back to turquoise on the second htr. 1 htr into each of the next 13 htr. Ch 2. Turn.

**Row 10—22**: Continue in the same way as row 9 following the heart pattern on the chart.

**Row 23—28**: Using turquoise only, repeat row 2 as for back. Fasten off.

## RIBBED CUFF

**Note** The ch 1 is not counted as a dc in this pattern.

In turquoise, ch 21, leaving a tail for sewing.

**Row 1**: Dc into second ch from hk and into each ch across. Turn [20dc].

**Row 2**: Ch 1; 1 dc in back lp only of first 10 dc. Turn.

**Row 3**: Ch 1; 1 rdcr in each of the 10 worked in row 2. Turn.

**Row 4**: Ch 1; 1 dc into both lps of each dc made in the last row, and into the unused 10 dc created in row 1. Turn [20dc].

**Row 5**: Ch 1; 1 dc into both lps of each dc across. Turn [20dc].

Repeat rows 2—5 11 times more.

Repeat rows 2—4 once more.

(There should be 14 raised ribs.)

Fasten off leaving a long tail for sewing up. Sew the shorter sides together. This is the back of the cuff. Fold over so that the ribbing is visible, like a polo neck collar.

## MAKING UP

The cosy is crocheted together on the right sides.

1  Place the front and back together with wrong sides together.

2  Pin a marker in the centre of the front between sts 14 and 15 at the top of the cosy. Count out 6 sts from the edge. Join in yarn and dc in the same stitch as joining. Dc in each st across and work 3 dc in the corner.

3  Continue to dc down the sides and across the bottom with 3 dc in each corner. Finish 6 sts in from the last corner leaving an opening for the ribbed cuff. (To keep the cosy flat, it may be necessary to work 2 dc in some of the sts down the side.)

4  Turn the cosy inside out and weave in all the ends.

5  Place the ribbed cuff inside the neck opening, making sure that the right side of the folded-over raised rib cuff is against the right side of the cosy.

6  Set the centre seam of the ribbed cuff at the centre of the back of the cosy. Ease the cuff gently to fit—it should not be necessary to stretch it too much. Pin in place. Using the long tail seam with an overhand stitch all the way round.

7  Weave in ends. Turn the cosy to the right side.

8  Insert the empty hot water bottle into the cosy by folding its sides over gently and easing it through the cuff opening.

*Hot Heart Cosy*

## STOPPER CORD

Using red, thread the stopper onto the yarn. Ch 25. Pull stopper to hk, ch 1, the stopper is now in place, sl st into each ch across [25 sl st]. Fasten off and use ends to sew to hole on the back of the neck of the hot water bottle.

## BLOCKING

It is not necessary to block this item using the yarn as specified. If you would like to block the piece then insert the hot water bottle into the cosy. Fill with hot water, then using a water-filled spray-mister dampen the cosy all over. Use your fingers to stretch and straighten the cosy into place. Set aside to dry.

## VARIATION

The yarn used in this pattern is a DK, but is quite thick. See the guide at the back of the book to find a suitable alternative, using the WPI as a comparison.

Use the tension to adjust your hook size accordingly or else add an even number of stitches to the rows across. If you need to adjust the length of the cosy, do the back first to check the size. If you need to make more rows, consider the placement of the heart design on the front as it is not set equidistant from the top and the bottom of the cosy.

## NATALIE'S NOTES

I love the variation and colour of this hand-dyed yarn. Luckily for us the internet has allowed us access to smaller companies like the one featured here, Colourspun.

Hand-dyed yarns are often sold in skeins. Unwind and roll into balls using the backs of chairs to hold the skein and prevent the yarn from tangling.

# ICE CREAM SUNDAE

This is a fun sculptural piece. Three balls of 'ice cream', chocolate and cherries are stitched, then glued in place. It's pure, delightful, yummy fun.

## MATERIALS

**Yarn**: Only small amounts of yarn are needed of Sirdar Snuggly Baby Bamboo DK, 50 g (1¾ oz) balls.

- Cream, col no 131 (Cream) for ice cream
- Perky pink, col no 124 (Pink) for ice cream
- Babe, col no 134 (Lilac) for ice cream

Rowan Cotton Glace, 50 g (1¾ oz)

- Toffee, col no 843 (Chocolate) for chocolate sauce and wafer
- Oyster, col no 730 (Biscuit) for wafer
- Poppy, col no 741 (Red) for cherry

Peter Pan Cupcake, 100 g (3½ oz)

- Col no 800 (White) for cream

Wool sewing needle

Scissors

Stuffing

Cardboard

Ice cream sundae glass

**Hooks**: 3.5 mm and 2 mm

## TENSION

Tension is important so that you achieve enough tightness so the stuffing does not show.

## FINISHED SIZE

Each ball measures about 4.5 cm (1¾ in) in diameter. The wafer measures 8 x 3 cm (3 x 1¼ in).

## SPECIAL PATTERN STITCH

**Dc2tog = Double crochet decrease** insert hk into specified st, yo and draw through, insert hk into next st, yo and draw through, yo and draw through all 3 lps on hk (decrease made).

## PATTERN

Each part of the pattern uses a different hook size.

## ICE CREAM BALLS

Using a 3.5 mm hk, make 3, one each in cream, pink and lilac.

**Row 1**: Ch 2; into second ch from hk make 12 dc. Join with sl st to first dc.

**Row 2**: Ch 1; 1 dc into same sp as joining; 2 dc into next dc; (1 dc into each of next 3 dc, 2 dc into next dc) twice; 1 dc into next 2 dc. Join with sl st to first dc [15dc].

**Row 3**: Ch 1; 1 dc into same sp as joining; 2 dc into next dc; (1 dc into each of next 4 dc, 2 dc into next dc) twice; 1 dc into next 3 dc. Join with sl st to first dc [18dc].

**Row 4**: Ch 1; 1 dc into same sp as joining; 2 dc into next dc; (1 dc into each of next 5 dc, 2 dc into next dc) twice; 1 dc into next 4 dc. Join with sl st to first dc [21dc].

**Row 5**: Ch 1; 1 dc into same sp as joining; 2 dc into next dc; (1 dc into each of next 6 dc, 2 dc into next dc) twice; 1 dc into next 5 dc. Join with sl st to first dc [24dc].

**Row 6**: Ch 1; 1 dc into each dc round. Join with sl st to first dc [24dc].

**Row 7**: Ch 1; 1 dc into same sp as joining; dc2tog over next 2 dc; (1 dc into each of the next 6 dc, dc2tog) twice; 1 dc into next 5 dc. Join with sl st to first dc [21dc].

**Row 8**: Ch 1; 1 dc into same sp as joining; dc2tog; (1 dc into each of the next 5 dc, dc2tog) twice; 1 dc into next 4 dc. Join with sl st to first dc [18dc].

**Row 9**: Ch 1; 1 dc into same sp as joining; dc2tog; (1 dc into each of the next 4 dc, dc2tog) twice; 1 dc into next 3 dc. Join with sl st to first dc [15dc].

**Row 10**: Ch 1; 1 dc into same sp as joining; dc2tog; (1 dc into each of the next 3 dc, dc2tog) twice; 1 dc into next 2 dc. Join with sl st to first dc [12dc].

**Row 11**: Ch 1; 1 dc into each dc round. Join with sl st to first dc. Fasten off [12dc].

Stuff each ball lightly but firmly so that they are spongy-soft. Use the tail length to close up the ball using a running stitch and weave in ends.

## CHOCOLATE SAUCE

You can have fun with this and alter the patterns if you want more drippings to the chocolate.

In chocolate, using a 2 mm hk, ch 2.

**Row 1**: 10 dc into second ch from hk. Join with sl st to first dc.

**Row 2**: Ch 1 (does not count as dc); 2 dc into each dc. Join with sl st to first dc [20dc].

**Row 3**: Ch 1; 1 dc into each dc. Join with

sl st to first dc [20dc].

**Row 4**: Ch 1; 1 dc into same dc as joining; 1 dc into next dc; sl st into next dc, 1 dc into next dc; ch 4; (and now working back on the 4 ch), 1 dc into second ch from hk and into next 2 ch; 1 dc into each of the next 5 dcs; ch 6; (and now working back on the 6 ch), 1 dc into second ch from hk and into each of the next 4 ch; 1 dc into next 6 dcs; ch 7; 1 sl st into second ch from hk; 1 dc into each of the next 5 ch; 1 dc into each of the next 5 dc. Join with sl st to first dc.

**Row 5**: Ch 1; 2 dc into same dc as joining; ch 2; 1 dc into second ch from hk; sl st into next dc; sl st into the 3 unused lps on first 4 ch 'drip' made in previous row; ch 1; sl st into next dc; 1 dc into each of the next 4 dc (2 on the drip, 2 on main body), sl st into next 2 dc; and 1 dc into each of next 5 unused lps of next 6 ch 'drip' from previous row; 2 dc into sixth ch of 'drip'; 1 dc into each of the next 5 dc; sl st into next dc; 1 dc into each of the next 2 dc; 1 sl st into each of the next 2 dc; 1 sl st into each of the next 6 unused lps of the 7 ch 'drip' from previous row; 1 sl st into seventh ch; 1 sl into next sl st; 1 sl st into each of the next 7 dcs; 1 dc into next dc; 1 sl st into each of next 2 dc and into beg dc. Fasten off leaving a long tail.

## CREAM MOTIF A

This is the motif used at the bottom of the sculpture and between the Ice Cream Balls to fill the space. Make 2 using a 3.5 mm hk.

In white, ch 6. Join with sl st to form a ring.

**Row 1**: Ch 2 (counts as an htr here and throughout), 15 htr into ring. Join with a sl st to the second ch of beg 2ch [16htr].

**Row 2**: Ch 2; (5 htr into next htr; 1 htr into next htr) 7 times; 5 htr into next htr. Join with sl st to second ch of beg 2ch [48htr]. Fasten off. Weave in ends.

## CREAM MOTIF B (FOLD–OVER PIECE)

Make 1, using a 3.5 mm hk. Follow the pattern directions for Cream Motif A and continue as follows:

**Row 3**: Ch 2; 1 htr into same st as joining; (3 htr into next htr, 2 htr into next htr) 15 times. (You should be about two-thirds of the way around. Do not complete the round). Turn [77htr].

**Row 4**: Ch 3 (counts as a tr); 1 tr into each of the next 24 htr. Turn [25tr].

**Row 5**: Ch 2; (1 htr, 1 dc into next tr; sl st into next tr) 11 times; sl st into last tr. Fasten off. Weave in ends.

## CREAM MOTIF C (SHELL)

Make 1, using a 3.5 mm hk. Use this as a visible layer of cream where the frilly edge is needed.

**Row 1**: Ch 4 (counts as a base ch and 1 tr); 3 trs into fourth ch from hk. Turn [4tr].

**Row 2**: Ch 3 (counts as a tr); 3 trs into same st; 4 trs into each of the next 3 trs. Turn [16htr].

**Row 3**: Ch 1; 1 dc in same st; (ch 3, 1 dc into next tr) 15 times. Fasten off.

Weave in ends.

## WAFER

Make 2. In biscuit, ch 8.

**Row 1**: 1 htr into third ch from hk and into each ch across. Turn [6htr].

**Row 2**: Ch 2, (counts as a htr); 1 htr into each st across. Turn [6htr].

**Row 3**: Ch 2; 1 htr into each of the next 4 htr; 2 htr into last htr. Turn [7htr].

**Row 4**: Ch 2; 1 htr into each of the next 5 htr; 2 htr into last htr. Turn [8htr].

**Row 5**: Ch 2; 1 htr in each htr across. Turn [8htr].

**Row 6**: Repeat row 5 [8htr].

**Row 7**: Ch 2; 1 htr into each of the next 6 htr; 2 htr into last htr. Turn [9htr].

**Row 8**: Ch 2; 1 htr into each of the next 7 htr; 2 htr into last htr. Turn [10htr].

**Rows 9–10**: Repeat row 5 [10htr].

**Row 11**: Ch 2; 1 htr into each of the next 8 htr; 2 htr into last htr. Turn [11htr].

**Row 12**: Ch 2; 1 htr into each of the next 9 htr; 2 htr into last htr. Turn [12htr].

**Rows 13–14**: Repeat row 5 [12htr].

**Row 15**: Ch 1; 1 dc into same st; 1 htr into each of the next 10 htr; 1 dc into last htr. Turn.

**Row 16**: Ch 1; sk next htr; 1 dc into next htr; 1 htr into next htr; 1 tr into each of the next 4 htr; 1 htr into next htr; 1 dc into next htr; sl st into last st. Fasten off.

Cut a piece of lightweight brown card slightly smaller than the wafer pieces. Insert card and using chocolate yarn, edge the wafer in dc stitches evenly so that the wafer stays flat.

## CHERRIES

In red, ch 2.

6 dc into second ch from hk. Fasten off. Stitch closed catching the 6 dc up in a running stitch to make a tight ball. Leave enough thread to sew onto the top of the Ice Cream Balls.

## ASSEMBLY

Stitch the chocolate over the top of the balls of ice cream. Sew the cherries to the top of the chocolate. Weave in any ends.

The example made is glued into a 1930s sundae glass. If you would like your sculpture to be removable, follow the instructions below, but line the container with greaseproof paper (baking parchment) before assembly so that you can pop the assembled piece into place whenever you want to display it.

Arrange a piece of 'cream' at the base of the container and, using a few blobs of glue, set in place. Position the balls of ice cream, the wafer and the larger element of cream between the ice cream balls so that it appears to be rising out in delicious foamy waves. Glue the pieces to each other and use long dressmaking pins to set in place. Use cling film (plastic wrap) to cover the whole piece while it dries.

## VARIATION

To make different desserts, vary the colours of the yarn. The cream could be made in custard-coloured yarn, and the chocolate pieces could be made to look like pouring cream.

## NATALIE'S NOTES

This is lovely example of the versatility of crochet. It is easy to create yarn versions of real life things. If you have empty containers sitting on shelves, then adding a whimsical item full of colour and fun makes your display more interesting. It's not necessary to use yarns of exact colour matches to the real thing – just get reasonably close in overall colour and the texture of the crochet and our imaginations make the sculpture more realistic.

# BOHO PAISLEY TABLEMAT AND COASTER

Ever popular, the Paisley motif has been brought up to date in this contemporary tablemat and coaster design. Several small motifs are combined into these designs, so you can use them as you wish, creating your own freeform items, or follow the template.

**MATERIALS**

**Yarn**: Rico Essentials Cotton DK, 50 g (1¾ oz)
- 1 x col no 02 (Red)
- 1 x col no 04 (Dark Red)
- 1 x col no 63 (Yellow)
- 1 x col no 40 (Blue)
- 1 x col no 69 (Pale Orange)
- 1 x col no 68 (Salmon Pink)

Wool sewing needle

Scissors

**Hook**: 3 mm

**TENSION**

Tension is not important for this project.

**FINISHED SIZE**

Tablemat: 25 x 38 cm (8¾ x 15 in)

Coaster: 13 x 15 cm (5 x 6 in)

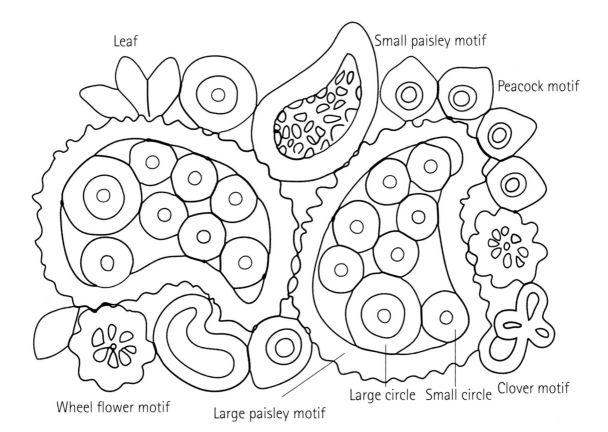

Leaf

Small paisley motif

Peacock motif

Wheel flower motif

Large paisley motif

Large circle    Small circle    Clover motif

## SPECIAL PATTERN STITCHES

**Htr2tog = Half treble decrease** Yo hk; insert hk into next st; yo and pull through; yo and insert hk into next st; yo and pull through, yo and pull through all 5 lps on hk.

**Dc2tog = Double Crochet Decrease**: Insert hk into specified st, yo and draw through, insert hk into next st, yo and draw through, yo and draw through all 3 lps on hk. (Decrease made).

**Trdec = Treble decrease:** Yo, insert hk into specified st, yo and pull through, yo and pull through 2 lps on hk, yo, insert hk into next st, yo and pull through, yo and pull through 2 lps on hk, yo and pull through remaining 3 lps.

## PATTERN

A number of individual motifs are joined by sewing together. The freeform placement of items and colours is your choice.

The Paisley motifs are worked as a flat length of chain and are not joined until after the first row. This stops the work from twisting.

## LARGE PAISLEY MOTIF

Make 2, ch 92.

**Row 1**: 1 htr into third ch from hk; 1 htr into each of next 8 ch; (2 htr into next ch, 1 htr into each of next 5 ch) 4 times; (2 htr into next ch, 1 htr in each of next 3 ch) 5 times; (2 htr into next ch, 1 htr into next ch) 4 times; 2 htr into next each of next 2 ch; 1 htr into each of the next 6 ch; (htr2tog over the next 2 ch; 1 htr into each of next 2 ch) twice; htr2tog over the next 2 ch; 1 htr into each of next 5 ch; (3 htr into next ch, 1 htr into next ch) twice; 1 htr into each of the next 2 ch [106htr].

Using the beg tail, sew the paisley together at the join and weave in ends.

**Row 2**: Join new col into joining st. Ch 1, 1 dc in same sp; 1 dc into next htr; (ch 2, sl st into side of dc just made) (picot made); 1 dc into each of next 3 htr; picot; continue round, and finish 1 dc into the last dc. Join with a sl st to the first dc. Fasten off. Use the end for sewing.

## FILLED PAISLEY MOTIF

Make 2 (1 for the coaster and 1 for the placemat). Ch 57.

**Row 1**: 1 htr into third ch from hk; 1 htr into next ch; (2 htr into next ch, 1 htr into each of next 3 ch) 3 times; 2 htr into next ch; 1 htr into each of next 4 ch; (2 htr into next ch, 1 htr into each of next 5 ch) twice; 2 htr into next ch; 1 htr into each of the next 7 ch; 1 tr into next ch; 1 dtr into next ch; 1 tr into next ch; 1 htr into each of the next 3 ch; htr2tog over the next 2 ch; 1 htr into next ch; htr2tog over the next 2 ch; 1 htr into next 2 ch; htr2tog over next 2 ch; 1 htr into last ch. Using the beginning tail, sew the paisley together at the join and weave in ends.

**Row 2**: Ch 1, 1 dc in same sp as joining; 1 dc into each of next 9 htr; ch 1; 1 dc into each of next 5 htr; ch 1; 1 dc into each of next 7 htr; ch 1; 1 dc into each of next 6 htr; ch 1; (1 dc into each of next 4 htr; ch 1) twice; 1 dc into each of next 6 htr; ch 1; 1 dc into each of next 3 htr; ch 1; 2 tr into next htr; ch 1; 1 dtr into next tr; work (1 dtr, 2 ttr, 1 dtr) into next dtr; 1 dtr into next tr; ch 1; 2 tr into next htr; ch 1; 1 dc into each of next 3 htr; dc2tog over next 2 htr; 1 dc into each of next 4 htr. Join with sl st to first dc. Fasten off.

**Centre Mesh**: This is worked in a random manner. In colour of your choosing, join with a sl st to the unused lp from the foundation ch (in the centre of the motif), starting close to the narrowest part of the Paisley but not in the centre of it. Ch 4; dc into an unused lp

3 to 4 stitches to the left; ch 4. Continue to work around the unused lps until you reach the starting position. (There is no need to be precise, the idea is to keep it freeform.) Dc into the first lp; ch 4; dc into next lp. Continue around in a spiral until you have filled the centre.

Weave in centre ends, and leave the outer colour for sewing.

## SMALL PAISLEY MOTIF

Ch 41.

**Row 1**: Into fourth ch from hk work 2 tr; 1 tr into each of next 5 ch; 2 tr into next ch; 1 tr into each of next 3 ch; 2 tr into next ch; 1 tr in each of next 3 ch; ch 1; 2 tr into next ch; 1 tr into each of next 3 ch; 2 tr into next ch; ch 1; 1 tr into each of the next 3 ch; 2 tr into each of next 3 ch; 1 tr into next ch; 2 tr into each of next 2 ch; 1 tr into each of the next 3 ch; (trdec over the next 2 ch) 3 times; 1 tr into last ch. Fasten off.

Using the beginning tail, sew the paisley together as before, stitching the fifth chain of beg ch securely to the last tr. Leave ends for sewing.

## PEACOCK EYES

Make 5. Ch 8, join with a sl st to form a ring.

**Row 1**: Ch 1 (does not count as a dc); 20 dc into ring. Join with sl st to first dc. Fasten off. Weave in ends.

**Row 2**: Join with new col into any st. Ch 1, 1 dc into same sp as joining; 2 dc into next dc; 1 dc into next dc; 2 htr into next dc; 1 htr into next dc; 2 htr into next dc; 1 tr into next dc; 2 tr into next dc; 1 tr into next dc; ch 1; 2 dtr into next dc; ch 1; 1 tr into next dc; 2 tr into next dc; 1 tr into next dc; 2 htr into next dc; 1 htr into next dc; 2 htr into next dc; 1 dc into each of next 3 dc; 2 dc into last st. Join with sl st to first dc. Fasten off. Leave tail ends for sewing. Weave in the centre colour ends.

## WHEEL FLOWER

Make 2. Ch 4.

**Row 1**: Ch 4 (counts as a tr and a 2 ch); (1 tr into ring; ch 2) 7 times. Join with sl st to second ch of beg 4ch [8 trs, 8 2ch sps].

**Row 2**: Sl st into 2ch lp; ch 1; work (1 dc, 1 htr, 1 tr; 1 dtr; 1 tr; 1 htr; 1 dc) into each 2ch sp around. Join with sl st to first dc. Fasten off. Leave ends for sewing.

## CLOVER LEAF

Make 2. Ch 13.

**Row 1**: 1 dc into second ch from hk; 1 dc into next ch; (2 dc into next ch; 1 dc into each of next 2 ch) three times; 1 dc into last ch.

**Base Points**: Ch 2; 1 dc into second ch from hk (these 2 ch are the Base Point and the dcs are worked into the sp formed); ch 7; 1 dc into Base Point; ch 9; 1 dc into Base Point ch; ch 7; 1 dc into Base Point. Sl st into base of last dc at end of row 1. Turn.

**Row 2**: Working into the first 7ch lp work 10 dc; work 13 dc into the next 9ch lp; and 10 dc into the last lp. Join with sl st to last dc made before 2ch sp was made. Fasten off. Use ends for sewing.

## SMALL CIRCLES

Make 14.

Ch 4. Join with sl st to form a ring.

**Row 1**: Ch 2 (counts as a tr); 23 tr into ring. Join with sl st to second ch of beg 2ch. Fasten off [24tr].

## LARGE CIRCLES

Make 3 using two colours.

Ch 4. Join with sl st to form a ring.

**Row 1**: Work as row 1 of Little Circles.

**Row 2**: Ch 2; (2 tr into next tr, 1 tr into next tr) 23 times; 2 tr into last tr. Join with sl st to second ch of beg 2ch. Fasten off [36tr].

Weave in the centre colour ends.

## LEAVES

Make 6. Ch 10.

**Row 1**: 1 dc in second ch from hk; 1 dc into each of next 3 ch, 1 htr into next ch; 2 tr into each of next 2 ch; 1 htr into next ch, work (1 dc, 2 htr, 1 dc) into last ch; rotating work and using the unused lps work: 1 htr into next lp; 2 tr into each of next 2 lps; 1 htr into next lp; 1 dc into each of next 3 lps; sl st into last lp. Fasten off. Use ends to sew in place.

## ASSEMBLY

Set your motifs following the diagram as a guide or to your own design. Arrange the motifs alongside each other until you are happy with the position. Begin with a Large Paisley motif and pin the next motif to it ensuring it lies flat. Sew together using the tail ends. Pass the needle underneath the V of the stitch in the adjoining motif, and then around to the next V, pass through that and repeat the process on the starting motif. Check the design before adding the next motif. The Paisley motifs are flimsy so need to be surrounded with firmer motifs surrounding them to keep the placemat and coaster firm.

It is not necessary to block this project.

## VARIATION

A larger table centre piece would look equally stunning in monochrome.

## NATALIE'S NOTES

The Paisley motif has been popularised in Scotland and the motif is named after the town of Paisley where cloth featuring this design was made.

This openwork cloth is fun to make, and although a little fiddly to put together it is much easier than it looks.

# CARNIVAL BUNTING

Cheerful and fun and so easy to make, you'll find it difficult to stop making them. And there are so many different options.

## MATERIALS

**Yarn:** Stylecraft Special DK, 100 g (3½ oz)
- Magenta, col no 1084 (Deep pink)
- Turquoise, col no 1068 (Turquoise)
- Aspen, col no 1422 (Sea blue)
- Citron, col no 1263 (Pale yellow)
- Shrimp, col no 1132 (Orange)
- Lavender, col no 1188 (Lavender)
- Lipstick, col no 1246 (Dark red)
- Fondant, col no 1241 (Pink)
- Pomegranate, col no 1083 (Rose)
- Meadow, col no 1065 (Green)
- Sunshine, col no 1114 (Bright yellow)

Wool sewing needle

Scissors

22 buttons, each about 20–25 mm (¾–1 in) in diameter

**Hook:** 4 mm

## TENSION

Each triangle is 15 cm (6 in) from top to point. It is important to work a little loosely as acrylic yarn does not easily lie flat if the tension is too tight. The bunting should drape a little.

## FINISHED SIZE

If you are making the garland with 11 triangles the total length is about 3.8 m (4 yd).

## PATTERN

Each triangle is made with a main colour and then edged with another. Make 11 as follows:

| Main Colour | Border Colour |
| --- | --- |
| Deep pink | Turquoise |
| Sea blue | Pale yellow |
| Orange | Lavender |
| Dark red | Pink |
| Pale yellow | Rose |
| Lavender | Dark red |
| Green | Sea blue |
| Pink | Bright yellow |
| Rose | Green |
| Bright yellow | Deep pink |
| Turquoise | Orange |

## TRIANGLE

With main colour, 4 ch.

**Row 1**: 3 tr into fourth ch from hk. Turn.

**Row 2**: Ch 2 (counts as a tr here and throughout); 1 tr into sp between next 2 tr; 2 tr into sp between next 2 tr; 1 tr into last sp, 1 tr into last treble. Turn [6tr].

**Row 3**: Ch 2; 1 tr in each sp across (working between the trs); 1 tr in last tr; turn [7tr].

**Rows 4–10**: Repeat row 3 10 more times. The number of trs made will increase by 1 on each row. By the last row you will have 17 trs.

Fasten off leaving ends about 20 cm (8 in) long.

## BORDER

With border colour, leaving a 20 cm (8 in) tail, join with dc in top corner and work down the side of the triangle: (ch 1, 1 dc) into each row 11 times (12 dc); ch 1, 3 dc into last side sp, 2 ch, 3 dc into next sp (on other side of triangle); (ch 1, 1 dc) up the side 12 times. Fasten off leaving a 20 cm (8 in) tail.

## GARLAND STRIP

**Foundation row**: In green, make a dcfc about 3.8 m (4 yd) long (see Techniques). (The exact number of stitches required is 426, but it is easier to make each row from one direction and unravel or add more stitches as required. Leave a tail in case you need to make a few more stitches.) To make a dcfc see Techniques.

**Row 1**: Starting from the beg end, join with green, ch 2, 1 htr into the large lp of each dcfc all the way across.

**Row 2**: In blue and starting from the beg end again, join with dc into beg 2ch; 1 dc between each of the next 34 htrs. Set the first triangle underneath the garland strip with wrong sides together. (The top end thread of triangle will be on the right-hand side.) Make 1 dc between each of the next 16 sts through both the garland strip and the triangle. Make 1 dc between each of the next 18 sts. Attach the next triangle as before. When you have attached all the triangles, 1 dc between each of the last 34 sts; make 1 dc into last htr. Fasten off.

## BLOCKING AND STARCHING

Lightly steam block several times. Spray with starch to set and stiffen a little. More than one application of spray starch may be required.

## NATALIE'S NOTES

I just love bunting and this pattern has several uses, children's rooms being an obvious choice. The lovely bright colours of the acrylic yarns makes it fun to make and it works up quickly. Acrylic does not always lie flat – if you are struggling to make the item lie flat, sew a little bead at the apex of each triangle to give it a little weight and allow gravity to pull it straight.

## VARIATION

This pattern is easily adapted to different scales—card embellishments being an obvious choice. Use lightweight-crochet thread and a small size hook to make strips for birthday and Christmas cards.
Or make a bunting in cream and white cottons, and embellish it with flowers (such as the ruffle flower from the Black Cat Doorstop) for a feminine effect.

## FINISHING

Unravel unused thread and secure ends of first two rows of garland strip.
Using the two ends of triangle border colour, stitch a button to the right side of each bunting triangle to cover the point where the triangle joins the garland strip. Weave in all ends.

Carnival Bunting

# petal seat pads

Bright and chunky doily-style seat pads with raised petal edges are made in pure wool and felted in the washing machine. They are really very easy and quick to make.

## MATERIALS
**Yarn**: Rowan Big Wool 50 g (1¾ in)
6 x Glamour, col no 26
(Makes 2 seat pads).
Wool sewing needle (super size)
Scissors
**Hook**: 12 mm

## TENSION
Tension is not critical in this project.

## FINISHED SIZE
Before felting project measures about 56 cm (22 in). After felting, each pad measures approximately 38cm (15 in) in diameter.

## SPECIAL PATTERN STITCHES

**Beg cl = Beg dtr cluster**: Ch 3, keeping the last lp on hk make 3 dtr into next tr, make 1 dtr in the next tr. Yo and draw through all 5 lps on hk.

**CL = Cluster**: Keeping the last lp of each dtr on hk, make 1 dtr into next tr, 3 dtr into the next tr, 1 dtr into the next tr. Yo and draw through all 6 lps on hk.

## PATTERN

The seat pad may pucker a little as you make it. Once it is felted it will pull straight.
Ch 2 at the beginning of each row acts as a tr or htr.

Using two strands of wool, ch 6. Join with sl st to form a ring.

**Row 1**: Ch 2, (counts as a tr); 14 tr into the ring. Join with sl st to the second ch of the beg 2ch [15tr].

**Row 2**: Beg cl; ch 8; (1 CL, ch 8) 4 times. Join with sl st into top of beg cl [5 8ch lps].

**Row 3**: Sl st into 8ch lp; ch 2; 9 htr into the same lp; (10 htr into the next lp) 4 times. Join with sl st to second ch of beg 2ch.

**Row 4**: Ch 2, 1 tr into same sp as joining; 1 tr into next htr; 2 tr into next htr; ch 4; (sk 4 htr, 2 tr into next htr, 1 tr into next htr, 2 tr into each of the next 2 htr, 1 tr into next htr, 2 tr into next htr, ch 4) 4 times; sk 4 htr; 2 tr into next htr; 1 tr into next htr; 2 tr into last htr. Join with sl st to second ch of beg 2ch.

**Row 5**: Sl st to next tr; ch 2; 1 tr into same sp; ch 1; sk 1 tr; 2 tr into next tr; ch 1; sk next tr; * ** into 4ch lp work (2 tr, ch 1, 2 tr, ch 1)**; (2 tr into next tr, sk 1 tr, ch 1) 5 times. Repeat from * 4 times; repeat from ** to ** once more; (2 tr into next tr, sk 1 tr, ch1) 3 times. Join with sl st to second ch of beg 2ch. [35 1ch lps].

**Row 6**: Sl st into next tr and into 1ch sp; ch 1, 1 dc in same sp; *(ch 3, 1 dc into next 1ch sp) 6 times [6 3ch lps]; ch 5 **; 1 dc into next 1ch sp; rep from * 3 times; rep from * to ** once. Join with sl st into the beg dc.

**Row 7**: Sl st in 3ch lp; ch 1; 1 dc in same sp; *(ch 3; 1 dc into next 3ch lp) 5 times; [5 3ch lps]; into 5ch lp work the following (1tr; 1 spike dtr into the base of one of the trs in row 5 that lie directly below the 5ch sp; 7 tr into 5 ch lp; 1 spike dtr into same place as the prev spike dtr; 1 tr) **; 1 dc in next 3ch sp; rep from * 3 times; rep from * to ** once. Join with sl st into the beg dc. Fasten off.

## FELTING

Weave in ends. Wash the seat pad in accordance with the instructions given in the Techniques section. Once it has felted, gently but firmly pull the pad into shape and pull up the 'petals' made by the spike stitches so that they stand up. Stretch out the lacy loops so that the holes are obvious.

## VARIATION

Try making funky matching placemats for the table using finer wool and a smaller hook.

## NATALIE'S NOTES

The fun of this pattern is the sense of expectation – you put the enormous, and rather floppy doily into the washing machine, switch the machine on and have an agonising wait while the item shrinks and felts. The piece should shrink by about a third and in this pattern the petals rise up because of the spike stitch in the last round.

With such thick thread it may be necessary to hold both the hook and the thread in a different way to your usual crochet technique.

# CHIRPY CHICK EGG COSIES

Cheeky and cheerful, egg cosies will bring a smile to any breakfast table. Easy to make, they are perfect for any time of year – not just Easter.

**MATERIALS**
**Yarn**: Rowan Fine Milk Cotton (4 ply) 50 g (1¾ oz)
- 1 x Bloom, col no 505 (Red)
- 1 x Midget Gem, col no 497 (Yellow)
- 1 x Waterbomb, col no 498 (Blue)
- 1 x Snow, col no 493 (White)

Sewing needle
Scissors
2 x mother of pearl buttons for each cosy
**Hook**: 2.5 mm
**FINISHED SIZE**
Each cosy measures 8 cm (3¼ in).

## BODY

Using main colour choice, ch 2.
**Row 1**: 5 dc into second ch from hk. Join with sl st into first dc.
(At the beg of each row ch 1– this starting ch does not count as a dc in this pattern.)
The first dc in each row should be made into the same st as joining.
**Row 2**: Ch 1; 2 dc into each dc. Join with sl st into first dc [10dc].
**Row 3**: Ch 1; 1 dc into each of the next 2 dc; 2 dc into the next dc; 1 dc in each of the next 4 dc; 2 dc in next dc; 1 dc into each of the next 2 dc. Join with sl st to first dc [12dc].
**Row 4**: Ch 1; 1 dc into each of the next 2 dc; 2 dc into the next dc; 1 dc into each of the next 2 dc; 2 dc into each of the next 2 dc; 1 dc into each of the next 2 dc; 2 dc into the next dc; 1 dc into each of the next 2 dc. Join with sl st to first dc [16dc].
**Row 5**: Ch 1; 1 dc into next dc; 2 dc into next dc; 1 dc into each of the next 2 dc; 2 dc into the next dc; 1 dc into each of the next 6 dc; 2 dc into the next dc; 1 dc into each of the next 2 dc; 2 dc into the next dc; 1 dc into the next dc. Join with sl st to first dc [20dc].
**Row 6**: Ch 1; 1 dc into each of the next 2 dc; (2 dc into the next dc, 1 dc into each of the next 4 dc) 3 times; 2 dc into the next dc; 1 dc into each of the next 2 dc. Join with sl st to first dc [24dc].
**Row 7**: Ch 1; 1 dc into each of the next 2 dc; (2 dc into the next dc, 1 dc into each of the next 4 dc) 4 times; 2 dc into the next dc; 1 dc into the next dc. Join with sl st to first dc [29dc].
**Row 8**: Ch 1; 1 dc in each dc. Join with sl st to first dc [29dc].
**Rows 9–19**: Repeat row 8.
Fasten off leaving a long tail. Weave in the beginning yarn and leave the long ending tail yarn for assembly.

## COMB

Using red, ch 7.
**Row 1**: Dc into third ch from hk; and into each ch to end. Turn [5dc].
**Row 2**: Ch 1, 1 tr into first dc, (1 dtr, 1tr) into next dc; sl st into same dc; sl st into next dc; ch 2; 1 tr into next dc; sl st into last dc.
Fasten off leaving a longer tail to sew up. Weave in starting end.

## BEAK AND CHEEKS

Using red and keeping a 30 cm (12 in) long end for sewing, ch 9.
**Row 1**: 6 dc into second ch from hk; sl st into each of the next 6 ch; 6 dc into last ch. Fasten off. Weave in end tail so that the 6dc group forms a rounded cheek to match the beginning cheek.

## TAIL

For each cosy make 3 in varying colours:
Ch 10–12, fasten off.
Place 3 tails together, double over and using the threads all together tie a tight knot so that the ch sts remain visible. Trim the ends of the threads to about 1 cm (¾ in).

*Chirpy Chick Egg Cosies*

## WINGS

Make 2 for each cosy.

Some of the cosies shown in the photograph have contrasting coloured wings and others have matching wings.

Ch 4, join with sl st to form a ring.

**Row 1**: Ch 2; 3 htr into ring; 2 tr; 1 dtr; ch 1; 1 dtr; 2 tr; 3 htr. Join with sl st to second ch of beg 2ch. Fasten off.

Weave in tail end, and leave a longer tail to attach wing to body.

## DRESSING THE CHICKS

1   Using the end thread from the body, sew the tails to the back of the cosy. Sew through the knot of threads allowing the ch st tails to stick up straight. Weave in ends. This is the back of the cosy.

2   Gently flatten the cosy and pin the comb to about 5 mm (¼ in) from the top and in line with the tails.

3   Using the long thread, sew up to the top of the comb along one side, and down again on the other. Weave in ends.

4   Double the beak over and stitch together just where the cheeks begin. Stitch to the front of the body about 5 or 6 rows down from the top with the cheeks hanging down.

5   Turn the cosy inside out and bring the needle and thread through. Lock the stitch in place by sewing through a loop of any stitch. Push the needle through the cosy in the place where you want to set the button for the eye. Stitch through once and lock the button firmly in place by locking the stitch on the wrong side as before. Bring the red thread back to the beak, inside the cosy and lock the stitch again. Set the second eye in place in the same way. Bring the thread back to the beak, lock it in place and weave in ends.

Make sure that you have got the 'eyes' firmly in place.

6   Attach the wings in place with dtr ends pointing slightly upwards and to the back of the cosy.

## NATALIE'S NOTES

These sunny little decorations are quick to work so make ideal gifts. They can be made in any colour to add wonderful accents to the breakfast table.

# Gypsy Cascade Tablecloth

A wildly colourful and extravagant doily-motif tablecloth that will make the ultimate statement. The colours are designed to cascade down the tablecloth starting in the centre with darker colours and ending with bright oranges and pinks.

## MATERIALS

**Yarn**: Patons 100 % Cotton 4-ply 100 g (3½ oz)

- 1 x Grape col no 1733 (Aubergine)
- 1 x Delta col no 1729 (Dark blue)
- 1 x Jade col no 1726 (Aqua green)
- 1 x Pomegranate col no 1724 (Red)
- 1 x Denim col no 1697 (Light blue)
- 2 x Kiwi col no 1703 (Green)
- 2 x Nectarine col no 1723 (Orange)
- 1 x Cheeky col no 1719 (Fuchsia)
- 2 x Candy col no 1734 (Pink)

Sewing Needle

Scissors

**Hook**: 3 mm

## TENSION

Using a 3 mm hook, the first three rows measures 7.5 cm (3 in).

## FINISHED SIZE

The finished cloth measures 155 cm (61 in) diameter, but it will stretch. Each motif measures 22cm (8½ in)

## PATTERN

There are 37 doily motifs in this tablecloth, and they are joined together to form a hexagonal shape. Each motif is made with rows of 5 colours. The colours are fastened off at the end of each row. The pattern explains how to make each doily motif and the chart below lists the colour combinations required. Make the centre row of motifs first and then the row to each side as you will find it easier to keep your place when joining. Written and chart instructions are given for this project

## COLOUR TABLE

The chart below gives the name of the motif, the number to make and the colours to use for the specified rows.

With colour 1, ch 6. Join with sl st to form a ring.

**Row 1**: Ch 2; 23 tr into ring (beg ch 2 counts as a tr) [24tr].

**Row 2**: Ch 4 (counts as first tr, and 2ch sp); (sk 1 tr, 1 tr into next tr, ch 2) 11 times. Join with sl st to second ch of beg

## PLACEMENT GUIDE

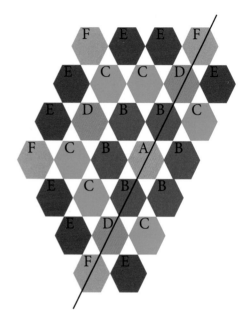

4ch (12 tr with 12 2ch sps).

**Row 3**: Sl st into 2ch sp; ch 2; 3 tr into same sp; ch 1; (4 tr into next 2 ch sp; ch 1) 11 times. Join with sl st into second ch of first 2 ch. Fasten off.

**Row 4**: Change to colour 2. 1 dc in previous 1ch sp to join of previous row; ch 2; (1 tr into next 1ch sp, ch 5, 1 tr into same sp,

## COLOUR TABLE

| Motif | No to make | Rows 1–3 | Rows 4–5 | Rows 6–7 | Rows 8–9 | Rows 10–11 |
|---|---|---|---|---|---|---|
| A | 1 | Aubergine | Light blue | Dark blue | Aqua | Green |
| B | 6 | Dark blue | Green | Light blue | Orange | Aqua |
| C | 8 | Aqua green | Orange | Red | Green | Pink |
| D | 4 | Aqua green | Aubergine | Orange | Green | Pink |
| E | 12 | Red | Green | Fuchsia | Pink | Orange |
| F | 6 | Aubergine | Green | Fuchsia | Pink | Orange |

*Gypsy Cascade Tablecloth*

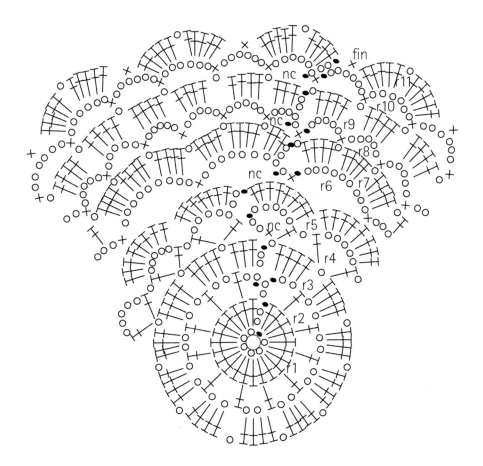

ch 1) 11 times; 1 tr into beg sp; ch 5. Join with sl st into second ch of first 2ch made. (If you are not changing colour at this point, ignore the dc and replace the beginning of the row as follows: rev sl st into prev 1ch sp, continue as for the rest of the pattern.)

**Row 5**: Sl st into next tr, and into 5ch lp; ch 2; 7 tr into 5ch lp (counts as 8 tr group); (8 tr into next 5ch lp) 11 times. Join with sl st into second ch of first 2 ch. Fasten off.

**Row 6**: Change to colour 3. Join with 1 dc between the fourth and fifth tr of the previous 8 tr group; (ch 9, 1 dc between the fourth and fifth tr of next 8 tr group) 11 times. Join with sl st into first dc [12 9ch lps]. (If you are not changing colour at this point then begin the row as follows: sl st into next 4 trs and into the sp between the fourth and fifth tr, ch 1, 1 dc in same sp, continue with pattern.)

**Row 7**: Sl st into next 9 ch lp; ch 2; 3 tr; ch 1; (4 tr, ch 1) twice into same sp; *(4 tr, ch 1) 3 times into next 9ch lp. Repeat from * 10 times. Join with sl st into second ch of first 2 ch. Fasten off.

**Row 8**: Change to colour 4. Join with 1 dc in

previous 1ch sp; ch 5; (dc in next 1ch sp, ch 5) 35 times. Join with sl st to first dc [36 5ch lps]. (If you are not changing colour at this point work as follows: rev sl st into prev 1ch sp; ch 1; 1 dc in same sp; continue as for the rest of the pattern.)

**Row 9**: Sl st in next 5ch sp; ch 2; 3 tr in same sp; ch 1; (4 tr into next 5ch sp, ch 1) 35 times. Join with sl st to second ch of first 2ch. Fasten off.

**Row 10**: Change to colour 5. Join with 1 dc in previous 1ch sp; ch 6; (dc in next 1ch sp, ch 6) 35 times. Join with sl st to first dc [36 6ch lps].

(If you are not changing colour at this point, work as follows: rev sl st into prev 1ch sp; ch 1; 1 dc in same sp; continue as for the rest of the pattern.)

**Row 11**: Sl st in next 6ch sp; ch 2 work (4 tr, ch 1, 5 tr) in same sp; 1 dc into next 6ch sp; (5 tr, ch 1, 5 tr into next 5ch sp, 1 dc into next 5ch sp) 17 times. Join with sl st to second ch of first 2ch. Fasten off.

### Join-as-you-go

Start with the first motif in the centre row as shown in the Placement Guide. To join the motif follow the pattern for row 11, and instead of making the ch 1, make 1 dc in the appropriate 1ch sp of the neighbouring motif. On beginning row 11, complee the first 'point' and then join the next 2 points to the neighbouring motif. The next point is not joined to any motif, and the next 2 are. In this pattern it is not necessary to join the motifs all in the same direction.

## FINISHING

Work in all threads. It is not necessary to block this item and it is recommended that you work in the threads once you have attached allthe motifs to ensure you have joined correctly.

## VARIATIONS

It is possible to make this tablecloth in just one colour and the pattern includes notes that explain what to do if you are not changing colour. It would look spectacular in white or ecru fine thread.

The centre of the pattern (rows 1-6) is also very pretty on its own and would make an attractive coaster.

## NATALIE'S NOTES

Using colour in crochet requires a great deal of conviction. In this tablecloth I have broken many of the 'rules' of colour. Creating a desirable colour combination requires some experimentation. Here, I have deliberately used clashing colours and then cooled things down with the greens and blues. The overall effect is vivid and full of life.

# HOT CHILLI RISTRa and STRING

A delightfully quirky decoration that is a bit of sculptural fun for the kitchen. It is also a great and satisfying introduction to the amigurumi technique of crochet.

## MATERIALS

**Yarn**: Stylecraft Special DK, 100 g (3½ oz)
- 1 x Lipstick, col no 1010 (Red)
- 1 x Khaki, col no 1027 (Green)

Wool sewing needle

Scissors

Raffia

Recycled stuffing (See Techniques)

**Hook**: 3 mm

## FINISHED SIZE

The chillies range from 8–10cm (3–4 in). They are gently stuffed.

## PATTERN

See Glossary for more about amigurumi.
The chillies are made from the top in a
continuous spiral with decreases made to
allow the chilli to gently curl asymmetrically
while narrowing down to a tip.

The main pattern is given below for the
largest chilli. Patterns for differently shaped
chillies, are given in the table opposite,
where the rate of decrease can be varied.

There is also a table of Shorthand Counted
Crochet for the pattern.

### HOT CHILLI BASIC PATTERN (A)

With red, ch 2.

**Row 1**: Into second ch from hk, and using
the bottom lp only, make 6 dc. Do not join in
this or any other rounds.

**Row 2**: 2 dc into each dc [12dc].

**Row 3**: 1 dc into each dc [12 dc].

**Row 4**: Repeat row 3.

**Row 5**: 1 dc into next 8 dc; dc2tog; 1 dc into
next 2 dc [11dc].

**Row 6**: 1 dc into each dc [11dc].

**Row 7**: Repeat row 6 [11dc].

**Row 8**: 1 dc into next 7 dc; dc2tog; 1dc into
next 2 dc [10 dc].

**Row 9**: 1 dc into each dc [10dc].

**Row 10**: Repeat row 9 [10dc].

**Row 11**: 1 dc into next 6 dc; dc2tog; 1dc
into next 2 dc [9dc].

**Row 12**: 1 dc into each dc [9dc].

**Row 13**: Repeat row 12 [9dc].

**Row 14**: 1 dc into next 5 dc; dc2tog; 1dc
into next 2 dc [8dc].

**Row 15**: 1 dc into each dc [8dc].

**Row 16**: 1 dc into next 4 dc; dc2tog; 1dc
into next 2 dc [7dc].

**Row 17**: 1 dc into each dc [7dc]. Stuff the
chilli at this point.

**Row 18**: 1 dc into next 3 dc; dc2tog; 1 dc
into next 2 dc [6dc].

**Row 19**: 1 dc into each dc [6dc].

**Row 20**: Dc2tog; 1 dc into next dc; dc2tog;
1 dc. Sl st into any visible stitch. Fasten off
pulling the chilli to a point. Leave a 20 cm
(8 in)-long tail for shaping.

Make 15 chillies for the ristra, or 12 chillies
for the string.

### OTHER SIZE CHILLIES CHART

Use this chart to vary the chillies slightly by
altering the pace of decrease. This will make
each chilli a little bit different. *See chart
opposite top.*

### SHORTHAND COUNTED LISTS

This is a shorthand version of the patterns
given above. For example: In chilli A, work the
first two rows as per pattern, then make 1 dc in

Hot Chilli Ristra and String

## OTHER SIZE CHILLIES CHART

|  | Chilli B | Chilli C | Chilli D |
|---|---|---|---|
| Row 1 | Row 1 [6 dc] | Row 1 [6 dc] | Row 1 [6 dc] |
| Row 2 | Row 2 [12 dc] | Row 2 [12 dc] | Row 2 [12 dc] |
| Row 3 | Row 3 [12 dc] | Row 3 [12 dc] | Row 3 [12 dc] |
| Row 4 | Row 3 [12 dc] | Row 5 [11 dc] | Row 3 [12 dc] * |
| Row 5 | Row 3 [12 dc] | Row 6 [11 dc] | Row 5 [11 dc] |
| Row 6 | Row 5 [11 dc] | Row 8 [10 dc] | Row 6 [11 dc] |
| Row 7 | Row 6 [11 dc] | Row 9 [10 dc] | Row 8 [10 dc] |
| Row 8 | Row 6 [11 dc] | Row 11 [9 dc] | Row 9 [10 dc] |
| Row 9 | Row 8 [10 dc] | Row 12 [9 dc] | Row 11 [9 dc] |
| Row 10 | Row 9 [10 dc] | Row 14 [8 dc] | Row 12 [9 dc] |
| Row 11 | Row 11 [9 dc] | Row 15 [8 dc] | Row 14 [8 dc] |
| Row 12 | Row 14 [8 dc] | Row 16 [7 dc] | Row 15 [8 dc] |
| Row 13 | Row 16 [7 dc] | Row 17 [7 dc] | Row 16 [7 dc] |
| Row 14 | Row 17 [7 dc] | Row 17 [7 dc] * | Row 17 [7 dc] * |
| Row 15 | Row 18 [6 dc] | Row 17 [7 dc] * | Row 18 [6 dc] |
| Row 16 | Row 19 [6 dc] | Row 18 [6 dc] | Row 19 [6 dc] * |
| Row 17 | Row 19 [6 dc] | Row 19 [6 dc] | Row 19 [6 dc] * |
| Row 18 | Row 20 [to 0] | Row 20 [to 0] | Row 20 [to 0] |

* denotes rows that can be easily omitted to make a shorter, smaller chilli.

## SHORTHAND COUNTED LISTS

| Chilli A | Chilli B | Chilli C | Chilli D |
|---|---|---|---|
| Start as for main pattern rows 1 and 2. Then continue as listed for each version. | | | |
| 32 dc, dec | 44 dc, dec | 20 dc, dec | 32 dc, dec |
| 31 dc, dec | 31 dc, dec | 20 dc, dec | 20 dc, dec |
| 28 dc, dec | 18 dc, dec | 18 dc, dec | 18 dc, dec |
| 25 dc, dec | 7 dc, dec | 16 dc, dec | 16 dc, dec |
| 14 dc, dec | 6 dc, dec | 14 dc, dec | 14 dc, dec |
| 12 dc, dec | 12 dc, dec | 26 dc, dec | 12 dc, dec |
| 8 dc | 14 dc | 8 dc | 14 dc, dec |
| Work row 20 as per pattern and finish off. | | | |

each of the next 32 dc, dc2tog. (You are now at the decrease in row 5 as shown in the pattern.) If you are using this shorthand pattern it is not necessary to use stitch markers. *See chart opposite bottom.*

## CAPS

Using green, make one cap for each chilli.
**Row 1**: Into second ch from hk work 7 dc, using the bottom lp. Do not join.
**Row 2**: 2 dc into each dc [14dc].
**Row 3**: 1 dc into first dc; 2 ch; (1 dc into next 2 dc, 2 ch) 5 times; 1 dc; sl st into last dc. Fasten off.

## SHAPING THE CHILLI

You may need to redistribute the stuffing by kneading it to get more into the tip.

The chilli will have a natural tendency to curl. Using the end tail and a wool needle, make two small stitches to secure the tip of the chilli, taking care not to distort its end. Slide the needle and thread in under the crochet and on the inside of the 'curl' of the chilli until about two-thirds up. Pull gently on the chilli and it should curl a little more tightly. Make a locking stitch. Stitch once more to the top of the chilli. Knot the long ends together making sure you place the knot as close as possible to the top of the chilli. Trim the ends to about 5 cm (2 in). Fasten off leaving a long tail for sewing the cap to the chilli and for attaching to the ristra or string.

## ADDING THE CAP

Using the long yarn end, stitch around the outer edge of the cap and then pull the yarn up to make it pucker. Then, place cap on top of the chilli, wrong side visible and stitch in place, tightening it as necessary and ensuring the red threads are tucked inside the cap. Pull the thread through to the top and tie (together with the beginning thread) a knot as close as possible to the top. Do not trim ends as you will use them to fix to a garland or onto a raffia plait.

## TO MAKE THE RISTRA RAFFIA PLAIT

Select enough raffia to make a rope about the thickness of your thumb. Bend the raffia over in the middle and twist to form a loop. Use another piece of raffia to bind the loop tightly. The loop should measure about 7.5 cm (3 in). Tie a knot securely. Catching the loose pieces of the raffia from below the knot, plait the raffia until the plaited strand measures about 12.5 cm (5 in) long. Plait firmly. Bind the base of the plait in the same way as you did for the loop. Trim the leftover ends of raffia to make a tassel about 10 cm (4 in).

Starting at the top of the plait, attach the chillies arranging the bigger ones towards the back and the smaller ones in front. Taper the number of chillies as you work down the plait. To attach the chillies to the plait, pull both loose threads through the raffia using a sharp wool needle. Once you have arranged them to your satisfaction, knot the ends together and to each other to look as if they have been tied into the plait. Spread some craft glue over the knots, allow to dry and then snip off the loose ends.

## TO MAKE THE STRING

Crochet a length of green ch to the length required. In the example shown here a length of 5.3 m (5¾ yd) was made. Double the chained string over so that you have two strands. Stitch the two lengths together about 2.5 cm (1 in) from the end to form a loop for hanging. Twist the chain lengths over a few times and then attach a chilli using the two long green ends and stitching through both chain lengths. Position the chillies at roughly equal intervals along the string. Match the end loop to that of the beginning by stitching the two chain ends together. If your chain is not equidistant, unravel one end until the distances are the same.

## NATALIE'S NOTES

In certain cultures the chilli is considered lucky. For instance, in Korea a string of chillies is hung outside a home where a new baby has been born. I love the idea of using them as decorations, with their bright red accent colour – just a lot of fun. .

# GRAFFITI DOOR PILLOW

Inspired by street art, this lively door pillow keeps the cold at bay while giving your home a cheerful splash of colour.

## MATERIALS

**Yarn**: Stylecraft Special) DK, 100 g (3½ oz)

- 1 x Turquoise, col no 1068 (Blue)
- 1 x Matador, col no 1010 (Deep red)
- 1 x Wisteria, col no 432 (Lilac)
- 1 x Citron, col no 1263 (Pale yellow)
- 1 x Meadow, col no 1065 (Green)
- 1 x Shrimp, col no 1132 (Orange)
- 1 x Fondant pink, col no 1241 (Pink)
- 1 x Violet, col no 1277 (Purple)
- 1 x Lipstick, col no 1246 (Bright red)
- 1 x Black, col no 1002 (Black)
- 1 x Cream, col no 1005 (Cream)
- 1 x Aspen, col no 1422 (Sea green)
- 1 x Saffron, col no 1081 (Bright yellow)

Wool sewing needle

Scissors

50 cm (20 in) close-weave fabric

500 g (17½ oz) sharp sand

1 m (39 in) wadding

**Hook**: 4 mm

## TENSION

Using a 4 mm hook, a 10 cm (4 in) square will require 17 stitches and 13 rows.

## FINISHED SIZE

98 cm (38.5 in) long x 19 cm (7.5 in) wide before stuffing.

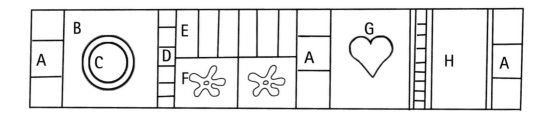

## PATTERN

The diagram above shows the layout of the different motifs. Leave a long tail for sewing when fastening off. Assemble the motifs as you make. Instructions for assembly are given after each pattern.

## STRIP 1, 2 AND 3 USING MOTIF A

Strips 1, 2 and 3 are each made up of three A motifs that are joined together at one end. Use the following colours:

**Strip 1**: Blue, deep red and lilac.
**Strip 2**: Pale yellow, green and orange.
**Strip 3**: Pink, purple and bright red.

## To Make Motif A

Ch 5. Join with a sl st to form a ring.
**Row 1**: Ch 4, (counts as an htr and 2ch sp) (4 htr into ring, ch 2) 3 times; 3 htr into ring. Join with sl st into second ch of beg 4ch.
**Row 2**: Ch 2 (counts as 1 htr); into next 2ch sp work (2 htr, ch 2, 2 htr); 1 htr into next htr; ch 1; sk 2 htr; *(1 htr into next htr; into next 2ch sp work (2 htr, ch 2, 2 htr); 1 htr into next htr; ch 1; sk 2 htr) Repeat from * twice more. Join with sl st into second ch of beg 2ch.
**Row 3**: Ch 2; 1 htr into each of the next 2 htr; into next 2ch sp work (2 htr, ch 2,

2 htr); 1 htr into each of the next 3 htr; *(ch 1; 1 htr into each of the next 3 htr; into next 2ch sp work 2 htr; ch 2; 2 htr; 1 htr into each of the next 3 htr) Repeat from * twice more. Join with sl st to second ch of beg ch. Fasten off leaving long tail for sewing.

## BASIC PATTERN

Several motifs as well as the back of the pillow are made using the basic pattern, with the only change being the number of rows or stitches.

Make the specified number of ch loosely.
**Row 1**: Into third ch from hk make 1 htr. Make 1 htr into each ch across. Turn. (The number of htr will be one less than the number of starting ch sts required.)
**Row 2**: Ch 2 (counts as an htr here and throughout); I htr into each htr across. Counting the first row, make as many rows as specified in the instructions.
Fasten off at the end of each motif.

## BACKGROUND SQUARE MOTIF B

Ch 32 [31 htr] then using the Basic Pattern make a square 25 rows deep. Fasten off. Using black, join the thread at the top left corner and edge the motif by making a dc in the side of each row. Fasten off, leaving long tails for sewing. Repeat for right-hand side of motif but not for the bottom or top. Sew to Strip 1 using black thread.

## CIRCLE MOTIF C

If you would like to use a chart for this motif instead of written instructions, refer to the pendulum disc pattern in The Folksy Flower Clock. Add more rows using the principle set dow in that pattern.

With green, ch 5. Join with sl st to form ring. (The starting 2 ch at the beginning of each row counts as 1 htr.)

**Row 1**: Ch 2; 11 htr into ring. Join with sl st to the second ch of beg 2ch [12htr].

**Row 2**: Ch 2; 1 htr into same st as joining sl st; 2 htr into each htr; join with sl st to the second ch of beg 2ch [24htr].

**Row 3**: Ch 2; 2 htr into next htr; *(1 htr into next htr, 2 htr into next htr). Repeat from * around. Join with sl st to the second ch of beg 2ch, changing colour to lilac through the sl st [36 htr].

**Row 4**: In lilac, ch 2; 1 htr into next htr; 2 htr into next htr; *(1 htr into each of the next 2 htr, 2 htr into next htr). Repeat from * around. Join with sl st to the second ch of beg 2ch. Changing colour to orange through the sl st [48htr].

**Row 5**: In orange, ch 2; 1 htr into each of the next 2 htr; 2 htr into next htr; *(1 htr into each of the next 3 htr, 2 htr into next htr). Repeat from * around. Join with sl st to second ch of beg 2ch. Changing colour to cream through the sl st [60htr].

**Row 6**: In cream, ch 2; 1 htr into each of the next 3 htr; 2 htr into next htr; *(1 htr into each of the next 4 htr, 2 htr into next htr). Repeat from * around. Join with sl st to second ch of beg 2ch. Changing colour to bright red through the sl st [72htr].

**Row 7**: In bright red, ch 1; 1 dc in same st as joining and 1 dc into each htr around. Join with sl st to first dc. Fasten off leaving a long tail for sewing [72dc].

Weave in ends of the circle, except for the final row. Sew the circle onto background square motif B, positioning the circle a little off-centre and to the left. Ensure that the motif is flat.

## MINI SQUARES MOTIF D

The left-hand edge of motif D is made up of 7 motifs, one in each of orange, purple, green, bright red, bright yellow, pink and sea green.

Ch 4. Join with sl st to form a ring.

**Row 1**: Ch 2; 2 tr into ring; ch 2; (3 tr into ring, ch 2) 3 times. Join with sl st to second ch of beg 2ch. Fasten off.

Sew each motif together in sequence.
In black, and starting at the top-left corner with right side facing, make 1 dc into each 2ch sp and into each tr stitch down the side of the strip. Repeat for other side leaving a long tail at each end for sewing. Do not stitch across the top and bottom of strip.
Sew Mini Squares Motif D to Background Square Motif B.

## STRIPED RECTANGLE MOTIF E

Using the Basic Pattern make a rectangle as follows:

In purple, ch 16.
Htr [15] for 5 rows. Change to new colour on the last st before turning. Work 5 rows in each of the following colours: purple, blue, pink, bright yellow, cream, bright red.
Fasten off.

## RECTANGLE OF SQUARES MOTIF F

Make two squares using the Basic Pattern, 1 in sea green and 1 in cream.
Ch 21. Htr [20] for 14 rows.
Sew the two squares together with rows running from left to right. Join to the bottom edge of Striped Rectangle Motif E with the purple stripe and the cream square on the left.

## HIPPIE FLOWERS FOR MOTIF F

Make 2, 1 in red and 1 in purple.
With yellow, ch 4. Join with sl st to form a ring.
**Row 1**: Ch 2 (counts as an htr); 14 htr into ring. Join with sl st to second ch of beg 2ch. Fasten off [15htr].
**Row 2**: (Foundation row of each petal) Join new colour into any htr. *Dc into htr; ch 6; 1 dc into second ch from hk; 1 dc into each of next 4 ch; 1 dc in each of next 2 htr. Rep from * around. Join with sl st into first dc. Turn the flower over so that in the next row you work back along the row just completed.

**Row 3**: *Working up petal and on unused lps of 6 ch from prev round, 1 dc in first lp; 1 htr into each of next 3 lps; into sp made by sixth ch in previous row work (3 tr, 1 htr, 3 tr); 1 tr into next dc; 1 htr into each of next 3 dc; 1 dc into next dc; sl st into each of next 2 dc (sp formed between petals); sk next dc. Repeat from * 4 more times.

Fasten off leaving a long tail for sewing the flower to the motifs.

Weave in centre ends.

Position the two flowers using the diagram as a guide so that the bright red flower sits in the centre of the left-hand cream square and the purple flower sits over the sea green square and Motif E. Stitch around the petals so that the flowers lie flat stretching them slightly to emphasise their shape.

Edge the large combined Motif E/F on the left and the right as before with black. Do not edge the top or the bottom.

Sew Motif E/F to the Mini Squares Motif D.

Edge Strip 2 of Motifs A in black on the right-hand side only and sew to side of Motif E/F.

## BLEEDING HEART MOTIF G

Using cream, make a square using the Basic Pattern.

Ch 26.

Htr [25] for 5 rows and then following the chart below create the heart with deep red. The heart is not symmetrical and is designed to twist as if hand drawn. Work another 5 rows of cream. Fasten off.

Using blue, join in any corner; 1 dc around the complete motif, making (1 dc, ch 1, 1 dc) in each corner. Fasten off.

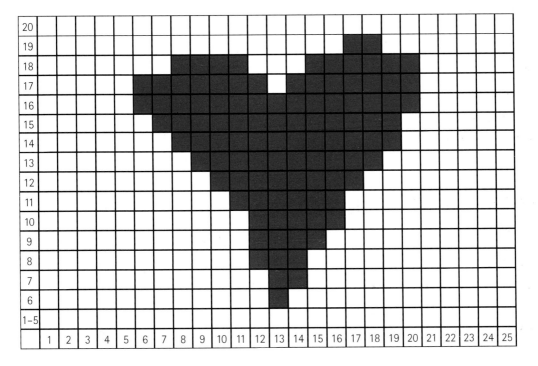

Sew Bleeding Heart Motif G to Strip 2 of Motif A.

## BLACK CHECK MOTIF H

With deep red, ch 32.

**Row 1**: Into third ch from hk make 1 htr. Make 1 htr into each ch across. Turn [31htr].

**Row 2**: Change to cream, ch 2 (counts as an htr here and throughout); 1 htr into each of the next 3 htr; change to black on the last part of the htr; 1 htr into each of the next 3 htr; carrying the cream thread behind your work, change to cream and make 1 htr into each of the next 3 htr. Continue in the same way to the end of the row, where you will end with 3 htr in black. Turn.

**Row 3**: Continue as for row 2, alternating colours after 3 htr, and ending the row with 4 htr cream.

**Row 4**: Repeat row 2.

**Row 5**: Repeat row 3.

**Row 6**: Change to red; ch 2, 1 htr into each htr across. Turn [31htr].

**Row 7**: Change to orange and repeat row 6.

**Rows 8–19**: Repeat row 6. Fasten off.

In black, work 1 dc in each st along the orange edge of the square.

## LITTLE CIRCLES FOR H

Make 4, 3 in bright yellow and 1 in blue.

Ch 5. Join with sl st to form a ring.

**Row 1**: Ch 1, (does not count as a dc); 12 dc into ring. Join with sl st to first dc. Fasten off leaving a long tail.

## PAISLEY MOTIF FOR H

In sea green, ch 18.

**Row 1**: 5 dc into second ch from hk; 1 dc into each of next 4 ch; 1 htr into each of the next 3 ch; 1 tr into each of the next 8 ch; 5 tr into last ch, rotating work and continuing up the unused lps of the beg 18ch; 1 tr into each of the next 5 lps; 1 htr into each of the next 4 lps; 1 dc into each of the next 2 lps; sl st into next 2 lps.

**Row 2**: Turn, and sl st into each of the prev 2 sl sts; 1 sl st into each of next 2 dc; 1 dc into each of next 3 htr; 1 htr into next htr, 1 htr into each of the next 3 tr; 1 tr into next tr; 2 tr into each of the next 6 trs; 1 htr into next tr; 1 dc into each of the next 5 trs; sl st into next tr. Fasten off and leave a long tail for sewing.

Position the Paisley motif and the little circles following the photograph as a guide and stitch in place around the edges, gently stretching the Paisley motif to emphasise its shape. Ensure that the motifs lie flat.

Sew Motif H to Motif G with the black-and-white check closest to the heart.

Sew strip 3 of Motifs A to the right-hand side of Motif G.

## BACK

The back is a stiped fabric made up of alternating colours, each 5 rows wide. Using your own choice of colours and following the Basic Pattern, ch 32.

Htr [31] for 5 rows. Change to new colour on the last st before turning. Work 5 rows of each colour for 120 rows. Fasten off. Weave in all ends.

## OUTER LINING

1   Cut 2 strips of lining 100 x 21 cm (39 x 8¼ in). Sew together along one long seam, open out and press the seam flat. Sew up the other long edge. Set aside.

## INNER LINING

1   Cut two pieces of close-grained fabric 95 x 8 cm (37½ x 3 in) and sew all around the edge. Fold this piece in half lenghwise to form a long tube and sew down the long edges. Double over the raw seam edges to prevent leakage of sand. Sew one narrow nd closed by doubling the seam. Fill with 500 g (17½ oz) of sharp sand. Sew the tube firmly closed.

2   Place the wadding inside the outer lining and then position the tube along the bottom long seam of the outer lining and tack in place. Add more stuffing until the pillow is full and the sand tube is surrounded.

**3** Sew up the side edges of the outer lining.

**4** Place the crocheted front and back pieces wrong sides together and with edges aligned. Starting in any corner crochet the two pieces together using a dc st. In each corner work (1 dc, ch1, 1 dc). Continue around until you reach the other short end. Insert the stuffed lining and then dc together to close the pillow. Fasten off and weave in ends.

## NATALIE'S NOTES

This is a great project to experiment with colour. The trick when using strong colours is to use those that may clash close to each other and then to use something more calming nearby. The black is used to outline and emphasise. Overall the effect is bright and harmonious. If you stick to this principle you will be able to create your own combination of colours. Never be afraid to combine colours that logically should not be harmonious at first glance.

  *Graffiti Door Pillow*

# HOPE BLANKET

Made in soft pastels, this luxurious blanket is one to stand the test of time — a blanket to be cherished and to be passed down within the family. Designed as a variation on the granny square and made of identical patches in differing colours, it is bordered with rows of contrasting colours. Simple but elegant.

## MATERIALS
**Yarn**: Rowan Belle Organic Aran
50 g (1¾ oz)
- 8 x Rose, col no 205 (Pink) A
- 4 x Robins egg, col no 209 (Blue) B
- 4 x Clementine, col no 215 (Orange) C
- 5 x Cut grass, col no 214 (Green) D
- 6 x Cilantro, col no 211 (Yellow) E
- 3 x Moonflower, col no 208 (Cream) F
- 3 x Orchard, col no 203 (Lilac) G

Wool sewing needle
Scissors
**Hook**: 5.5 mm

## TENSION
If the motifs are stitched with too loose a tension there will too much stretch. If they are stitched too tight they will not lie flat. Increase/decrease your hook size to suit your style of crochet.

## FINISHED SIZE
Each motif measures about 14 cm (5 ½in) square. The finished blanket measures 2 x 1.5 m (78 x 59 in)

## PATTERN

The blanket is made up of squares made in 7 colours and assembled in the order given in the diagram below right.

The join-as-you-go method is used (see Techniques).

A (pink) make 29
B (blue) make 16
C (orange) make 15
D (green) make 21
E (yellow) make 18
F (cream) make 12
G (lilac) make 6

Make 117 squares in all.

Ch 6 and join with sl st to form a ring.

**Row 1**: Ch 4 (first 2 ch counts as a tr); into ring work (4 tr, ch 2) 3 times; 3 tr. Join with sl st to second ch of beg 4ch.

**Row 2**: Ch 2 work (2 tr, ch 2, 2 tr) into next 2ch sp; 1 tr into next tr; ch 2; sk 2 tr; *1 tr into next tr; into next 2ch sp work (2 tr, ch 2, 2 tr); 1 tr into next tr; ch 2; sk 2 tr; rep from * twice more. Join with sl st to second ch of beg 2ch.

**Row 3**: Ch 2; 1 tr into each of the next 2 trs; into next 2 ch sp work (2 tr, ch 2, 2 tr); 1 tr into each of next 3 tr; ch 1; *1 tr into each of the next 3 trs; into next 2ch sp work (2 tr, ch 2, 2 tr); 1 tr into each of the next 3 trs; ch 1; rep from * twice more. Join with sl st to second ch of beg 2ch.

**Row 4**: Ch 2; 1 tr into each of the next 4 trs; into next 2 ch sp work (2 tr, ch 2, 2 tr); 1 tr into each of the next 5 trs; ch 2; 1 dc into ch sp from previous row, ch 2, *1 tr into each of the next 5 trs; into next 2ch sp work (2 tr, ch 2, 2 tr); 1 tr into each of the next 5 trs, ch 2; 1 dc into ch sp from prev row; ch 2, 1 rep from * twice more. Join with sl st to second ch of beg 2ch.

## JOINING ROWS

Join-as-you-go in row 4 at appropriate points to position your motif in the correct place. After turning the second corner of the motif join the corner: instead of working the ch 2 for the corner work ch 1, 1 dc into 2ch sp in adjoining motif, ch 1, continue working motif.

| | | | | | | | | | |
|---|---|---|---|---|---|---|---|---|---|
| A | B | A | B | A | B | A | B | A | 1 |
| C | D | E | D | C | D | E | D | C | 2 |
| A | F | G | F | A | F | G | F | A | 3 |
| D | E | C | E | D | E | C | E | D | 4 |
| A | B | A | B | A | B | A | B | A | 5 |
| C | D | E | D | C | D | E | D | C | 6 |
| A | F | G | F | A | F | G | F | A | 7 |
| D | E | C | E | D | E | C | E | D | 8 |
| A | B | A | B | A | B | A | B | A | 8 |
| C | D | E | D | C | D | E | D | C | 10 |
| A | F | G | F | A | F | G | F | A | 11 |
| D | E | C | E | D | E | C | E | D | 12 |
| A | B | A | B | A | B | A | B | A | 13 |

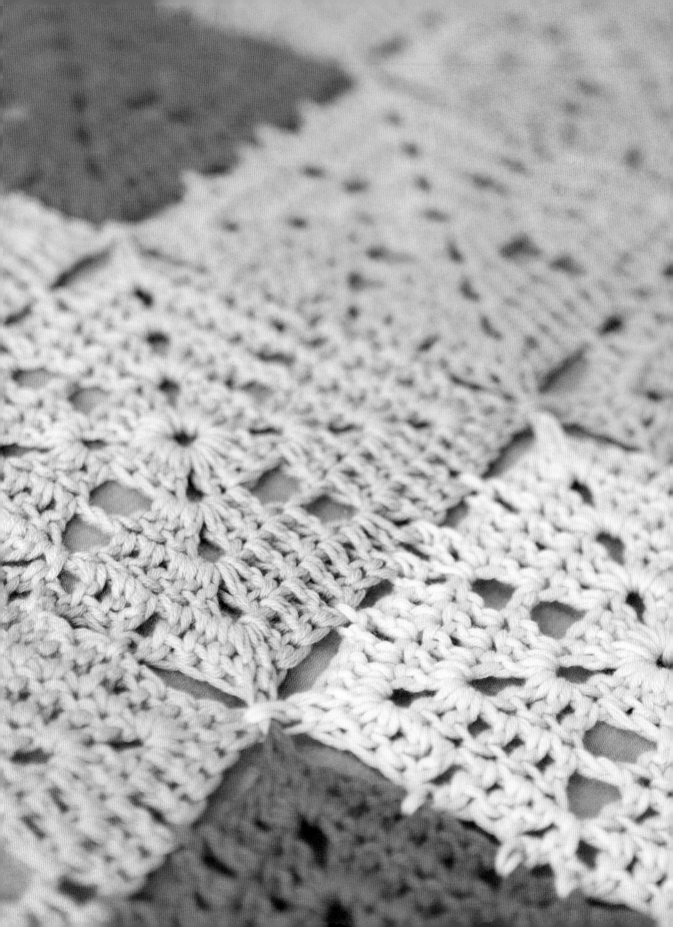

Join again with a dc after working the second tr in the next batch of 5 trs. Join again where you begin to form the V, working the last tr as usual, 1 dc in 2ch sp of adjoining motif, ch 1, 1 dc in ch sp, ch1 and join again in next 2ch sp of V st. Continue and repeat joins in the fourth tr of 5 tr and again in the corner. Continue to join on the next side.

## BORDER

**Row 1**: With lilac, join in any corner in 2ch sp, making sure that the work is right-side facing; 1 tr into next tr; ch 1; sk 1 tr; 1 tr into each of next 4 trs; ch 1; *sk 1 tr; 1 tr into each of next 2ch sps; ch 1; (sk 1 tr, 1 tr into each of next 4 trs, ch 1) 3 times; rep from * along the length of the blanket until you get to the last V section where you should make 1 tr into each of the 2ch sps, sk 1 tr; ch 1; 1 tr into each of the next 4 trs; ch 1; sk 1 tr; 1 tr into next tr; and into the corner work (2 tr, ch 2, 2 tr); 1 tr in next tr; ch 1; sk 1 tr; 1 tr into each of the next 4 tr; ch 1. Repeat from * until you

have completed the entire border. On the last corner make 2 tr into corner, ch 2, 1 tr. Join with sl st to second ch of beg 4ch.

**Row 2**: Ch 2; 1 tr into next tr; 1 tr into ch sp; ch 1; sk 1 tr; 1 tr into each of next 3 tr; ch 1; 1 tr into each of next 2 trs; ch 1; *1 tr into each of next 3 trs; ch 1; sk 1 tr, 1 tr into ch sp; 1 tr into each of next 4 trs; 1 tr into next ch sp; ch 1; sk 1 tr; 1 tr into each of next 3 trs; ch 1; 1 tr into each of next 2 trs; ch 1; rep from * along length of blanket until you reach the last motif and the end of a full pattern repeat, and then work as follows: 1 tr into each of next 3 trs; ch 1; sk 1 tr; 1 tr into ch sp; 1 tr into each of next 3 trs. Into corner 2ch sp work (2 tr, ch 1, 2 tr); then continue as follows: 1 tr into each of the next 3 trs; 1 tr into ch sp; ch 1; sk 1 tr; 1 tr into each of the next 3 trs; ch 1; 1 tr into each of the next 2 trs; ch 1; rep from * along the length of the blanket until you have completed the entire border; on the last corner make 1 tr into next tr. Join with sl st to second ch of beg 2ch.

**Row 3**: In pink, join into first tr next to beg

2ch from prev row; ch 2; 1 tr into next tr; 1 tr into ch sp; ch 1; sk 1 tr * 1 tr into each of next 2 trs and into ch sp; ch 2; 1 dc into sp between next 2 trs; ch 2; (V-st made); 1 tr into ch sp; 1 tr into each of next 2 trs; ch 1; sk 1 tr; 1 tr into next ch sp; 1 tr into next 2 trs; ch 2; sk 2 trs; 1 tr into next 2 trs; 1 tr into ch sp; ch 1; sk 1 tr; rep from * along the length of the blanket until you reach the next corner and have completed the full pattern rep. Work as follows: 1 tr in ch sp; 1 tr in next 2 trs, ch 1; sk 1 tr; 1 tr into each of next 3 trs; into corner work (2 tr, ch 2, 2 tr); 1 tr into next 3 trs; ch 1; sk 1 tr; 1 tr into each of next 2 trs; 1 tr into ch sp; ch 1; sk 1 tr. Repeat from * and continue until you have completed the entire border, ending with ch 1. Join with sl st to second ch of beg 2ch. Fasten off.

**Row 4**: With green, join into last st from previous row; ch 2; 1 tr into next tr; ch 1; sk 1 tr; 1 tr into each of next 3 trs; ch 1; sk 1 tr; *1 tr into each of next 2ch sps; ch 1; sk 1 tr; 1 tr into next tr, ch 1; sk 1 tr; 1 tr into ch sp; ch 1; sk 1 tr; 1 tr into each of next 2 trs; 2 tr into 2ch sps; 1 tr into each of next 2 trs; ch 1; sk 1 tr; 1 tr into ch sp; ch 1; sk 1 tr; 1 tr in next tr; ch 1; sk 1 tr rep from * until you have reached the next corner and continue as follows: 1 tr into each of next 2ch sps; (ch 1, sk 1 tr, 1 tr into each of next 2 trs, 1 tr into ch sp) twice; ch 1; sk 1 tr; 1 tr into each of next 4 trs. Into corner work (2 tr, ch 2, 2 tr); 1 tr into each of the next 4 trs, (ch 1, sk 1 tr, 1 tr into ch sp, 1 tr into

each of next 2 trs) twice; ch 1; sk 1 tr; rep from * and continue until you have completed the entire border ending with 1 tr into ch sp. Join with sl st to second ch of beg 2ch.

**Row 5**: Ch 3; sk 1 tr; 1 tr into ch sp and into each of next 3 trs; ch 1; *1 tr into each of next 2 trs; ch 1; (1 tr into next tr, 1 tr into ch sp) twice; ch 1; sk 1 tr; 1 tr into each of next 4 trs, ch 1; sk 1 tr; (1 tr into ch sp, 1 tr into next tr) twice; ch 1; rep from * until you have reached the next corner and continue as follows: 1 tr into each of next 2 trs, ch 1; 1 tr into each of next 3 trs; 1 tr into ch sp; ch 1; sk 1 tr; 1 tr into each of next 2 trs and into ch sp; (ch 1; sk 1 tr; 1 tr into each of next 2 trs) twice and into corner work (2 tr, ch 2, 2 tr); (1 tr into each of the next 2 trs, ch 1; sk 1 tr) twice; 1 tr into ch sp; 1 tr into each of next 2 trs; ch 1; sk 1 sp; 1 tr into next ch sp; 1 tr into each of next 3 trs; ch 1; and repeat from * and continue until you have completed the entire border ending with 1 tr. Join with sl st to second ch of beg 3ch.

**Row 6**: Sl st into ch sp; ch 2; *1 tr into each of next 4 trs; 1 tr into ch sp; ch 2; 1 dc into sp between next 2 trs; ch 2; (V-s made); 1 tr into ch sp; 1 tr into each of next 4 trs and into ch sp; ch 1; sk 1 tr; 1 tr into next 2 tr; ch 1; sk 1 tr; 1 tr into ch sp; rep from * along the length of the blanket until you reach the next corner and have completed the full pattern rep and work as follows: ch 1; sk 1 tr; 1 tr into each of next 2 trs; 1 tr in ch sp; 1 tr in next 2 trs and ch sp; ch 1; sk 1 tr; 1 tr into each of

Hope Blanket

next 3 trs; into corner work (2 tr, ch 2, 2 tr);
1 tr into next 3 trs; ch 1; sk 1 tr; 1 tr into ch sp
and into each of next 2 trs; 1 tr into ch sp;
1 tr into each of next 2 trs; ch 1; sk 1 tr; 1 tr
into next tr. Repeat from * and continue until
you have completed the entire border, ending
with ch 1. Join with sl st to second ch of beg
2ch. Fasten off

## FINISHING

It is not necessary to block this blanket
using the specified yarn. Weave in all ends
and steam press gently. Drape over a bed for
a few days to allow the yarn to settle before
using it.

## NATALIE'S NOTES

Blankets like this one remind me of the
days when young girls prepared for future
married life and created a 'bottom drawer' or
a Hope Chest, in the hope that they would
one day get married. Grandmothers and
mothers would all contribute by making and
collecting items. Today, a blanket like this is
ideal to give to a young child to snuggle up
in and to keep for many years, comforted by
the knowledge that family, or someone who
cared, made it especially for them.

# TReaSURe BaGS

Make these pretty little bags to hold and store precious things. Shown here in two colours, the treasure bag has a round base with easy-to-make mesh sides that will stretch and expand to fit the contents. Each is finished with a lace tie to close the bag and keep the contents safe.

**MATERIALS**
Yarn: Rowan Handknit Cotton DK, 50 g (1¾ oz)
- 1 x Gooseberry, col no 219 (Green)
- 1 x Slick, col no 313 (Pink)
Large eye sewing needle
Scissors
**Hook**: 3.5 mm
**TENSION**
Tension is not important for this bag.
**FINISHED SIZE**
The base of the bag measures 7 cm (3¾ in) and the overall height is 11.5 cm (4½ in).

## BASE

The starting 2 ch at the beginning of each row counts as a tr. (You may wish to use a 3 ch instead if it suits your tension as there is less stretch in this cotton yarn.) The crochet chart for this pattern appears at the base of this page.

Ch 5. Join with sl st to form ring.
**Row 1**: Ch 2; 11 tr into the ring. Join with sl st to the top of the starting 2ch [12tr].
**Row 2**: Ch 2; 1 tr into same sp as joining; 2 tr into each tr. Join with sl st to second ch of beg 2ch [24tr].
**Row 3**: Ch 2; (2 tr into next tr, 1 tr into next tr) 11 times; 2 tr into last tr. Join with sl st to second ch of beg 2ch [36tr].
**Row 4**: Ch 2; 1 htr into each tr, using back lp only. Join with sl st [36htr].

## FOUNDATION MESH ROW

Ch1; 1 dc in same sp; ch 3; 1 tr in same sp; sk 2 tr; *(1tr, ch 3, dc 1) in next tr; (1 dc, ch 3, 1 tr) in next tr; sk 2 tr; Rep from * 8 times; (1 tr, ch 3, 1 dc) into last tr. Sl st into first dc and into each of the 3 ch, and into top of first tr, and into the sp between the first and second trs [9 mesh bases].

## MESH PATTERN ROW

The mesh is worked in the sps between the 2 trs from the previous row and is referred to here as the sps.
Ch 2 (counts as a tr here) in starting sp between 2 trs; (1 tr, ch 3, dc 1, ch 3, 1 tr) in sp between the next 2 tr 8 times; in beginning sp (1 tr, ch 3, 1 dc, ch 3); join with sl st into third ch of starting ch; sl st into sp between first two trs.
Repeat mesh pattern row 5 more times (total 6 pattern rows).

## FINISHING ROWS

In this row the stitches are made in each of the 3ch lps.
**Row 1**: Sl st into tr, and into 3ch lp; ch 2 (counts as a tr); 1 tr in same 3ch lp; 2 tr in next 3ch lp and each 3ch lp around. Join with sl st into second ch of starting 2ch. (You should have 36 tr in 18 groups of 2 tr.) The gaps formed between the groups is where you will thread the lace.
**Row 2**: Rev sl st into sp between the 2 tr group, dc in same sp; (ch 6, 1 dc into sp between next tr grouping) 17 times; ch 6. Join with sl st into first dc [18 6ch lps].
**Row 3**: Sl st into 6ch lp; (1 dc, 1 htr, 1 tr, ch 1, 1 tr, 1 htr, 1 dc) into each 6ch lp around. Join with sl st into 1 dc. Fasten off and weave in ends.

## LACE TIE

In contrasting thread, make a double crochet foundation ch (See Techniques) 45 cm (18 in) long. Weave in ends. Thread the lace through row 1 of the Finishing Rows section. Tie a bow.

## VARIATION

You can make these treasure bags for Christmas or birthdays as gift bags. Use thread or yarn to match the colour of the season or the present. Use finer threads to make smaller bags, or even extend the mesh to make the bag taller. Add silver and gold filament thread to add a sparkly touch. Beads could be added for extra detail.

## NATALIE'S NOTES

The base of this bag is made using a basic crochet method for making a circle, increase on the first row by doubling the number of stitches. On the second row increase every second stitch, and on the third row, increase in every third stitch and so on. You could use the pattern in dc and htrs and adjust the starting number of stitches to suit your pattern and to keep the disk flat.

# THE FOLKSY FLOWER CLOCK

Inspired by the cuckoo clock this naïve country-style clock puts a fresh face on the iconic clock. Fun and contemporary, it will look great in kitchens, halls and children's rooms.

## MATERIALS

**Yarn**: Anchor Style Creativa Fino, 50 g (1¾ oz)

- Col no 1334 (Light blue)
- Col no 1323 (Dark blue)
- Col no 1329 (Purple)
- Col no 108 (Lilac)
- Col no 1330 (Green)
- Col no 1338 (Orange)
- Col no 1326 (Yellow)
- Col no 1333 (Red)
- Col no 1320 (Pink)

1 battery-operated clock mechanism

Stiff cardboard

Rectangular picture frame 17.5 x 13 cm (5 x 3 in)

Quick-drying fabric adhesive

Clothes pegs and/or dressmaking pins

25 cm (10 in) length of 6 mm (¼ in) dowel

Wool sewing needle

Scissors

Cardboard

**Hook**: 2.5 mm

## TENSION

Tension is not important for this pattern.

## FINISHED SIZE

20 x 16 cm (8 x 6¼ in) excluding pendulum

**Htr2tog = Half treble decrease**: Yo, insert hk into next st, yo, pull through, yo, insert hk into following st, yo, pull through, yo and pull through all 5 loops on hk (decrease made).

The clock is comprised of six main parts: main face (A), 3 fascias (B, C, and D), 2 pendulum discs (E), clock face disk (F), a pendulum (G) and door (H). Additionally there are several small motifs; the oak leaf, crazy daisy, gerbera, little leaf, purple flower and star flower.

Cut out the cardboard pieces according to the plan and test the pieces for fit.

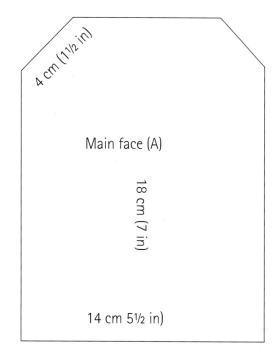

Main face (A)

4 cm (1½ in)

18 cm (7 in)

14 cm 5½ in)

## MAIN FACE (A)

Start at the narrow end (the top) when you make this piece and increase over 6 rows until it becomes straight and then continue. In blue, ch 28.

**Row 1**: 1 htr into third ch from hk (first 2 ch counts as an htr); 1 htr into each ch across. Turn [27htr].

**Row 2**: Ch 2 (counts as an htr here and throughout); 2 htr into next htr (increase made); 1 htr into each htr across until the penultimate htr, 2 htr into this htr (increase made); 1 htr into last htr. Turn [29htr].

**Row 3**: Repeat row 2 [31htr].

**Row 4**: Repeat row 2 [33 htr].

**Row 5**: Ch 2; 2 htr into each of next 2 htr; 1 htr into each htr across until the third to last htr, 2 htr into each of next 2 htr; 1 htr into last htr. Turn [37htr].

**Row 6**: Ch 2; 1 htr into each htr across. Turn [37htr].

**Rows 7–25**: Repeat row 6.

**Row 26**: Ch 2; 1 htr2tog over next 2 stitches; 1 htr into each st across until the third from last htr, htr2tog over the next 2 sts; 1 htr into last htr. Turn [35htr].

**Row 27**: Repeat row 26 [33 htr].

**Row 28**: Repeat row 26 [31 htr]. Fasten off. Weave in ends.

## FASCIA (B)

Rows 1–4 are repeated in reverse in rows 6–9 so that you make a complete covering for the fascia. (The rate of increase/decrease is repeated in reverse order.) When doubled on row 5 your piece should match on the other three sides. This principle is repeated for Fascia (C).

In blue, ch 29.

**Row 1**: 1 htr into third ch from hk (first 2 ch count as an htr); 1 htr into each ch across. Turn [28htr].

**Row 2**: Ch 2; 2 htr into each of the next 2 htr; 1 htr into each st across until the third from last htr, htr2tog over the next 2 sts; 1 htr into last htr. Turn [29htr].

**Row 3**: Ch 2; 1 htr2tog over next 2 sts; 1 htr into each st across until the third and second to last htrs, 2 htr into both of these; 1 htr into last htr. Turn [30htr].

**Row 4**: Ch 2, 1 htr into each st across until the third and second-to-last htrs, 1 htr2tog over the next 2 sts; 1 htr into last htr. Turn [29htr].

**Row 5**: Ch 2; 1 htr into each st across. Turn [29 htr].

**Row 6**: Ch 2; 1 htr into each st across until the penultimate htr, 2 htr into this htr; 1 htr into last htr. Turn [30htr].

**Row 7**: Ch 2; 2 htr into next htr; 1 htr in each st across and make a htr2tog in the fifth and fourth-to-last sts; work another htr2tog in the third and second to last sts; 1 htr into last htr. Turn [29htr].

**Row 8**: Ch 2; (1 htr2tog over the next 2 sts) twice; 1 htr into each st across until the penultimate htr, make 2 htr into this htr; 1 htr into last htr. Turn [28htr].

**Row 9**: Repeat row 5. Fasten off and leave long ends for sewing [29htr].

## FASCIA (C )

In blue, ch 23.

**Row 1**: 1 htr into third ch from hk (first 2 ch count as an htr); 1 htr into each ch across. Turn [22htr].

**Row 2**: Ch 2; 1 htr2tog over next 2 sts; 1 htr into each st across until the third and second to last htrs, 2 htr into both of these htrs; 1 htr into last htr. Turn [23htr].

**Row 3**: Ch 2; 2 htr into each of the next 2 htr; 1 htr into each st across until the third-from-last htr, htr2tog over the next

3 cm (1¼ in)

3 cm (1¼ in)

3 cm (1¼ in)

13 cm (5¼ in)

12 cm (4¾ in)

B

10 cm (4 in)

12 cm (4¾ in)

C

16 cm (6¼ in)

D

2 sts; 1 htr into last htr. Turn [24htr].

**Row 4**: Ch 2, 1 htr2tog over the next 2 htrs; 1 htr into each stitch across. Turn [23htr].

**Row 5**: Ch 2; 1 htr into each st across. Turn [23 htr].

**Row 6**: Ch 2; 2 htr into next htr; 1 htr into each st across. Turn [24htr].

**Row 7**: Ch 2; (htr2tog over next 2 sts) twice; 1 htr into each st across until the penultimate htr, 2 htr into this htr; 1 htr into last htr. Turn [23htr].

**Row 8**: Ch 2; 2 htr into next htr; 1 htr in each stitch across and work a htr2tog in the fifth and fourth to last sts; work another htr2tog in the third and second to last sts; 1 htr into last htr. Turn [22htr].

**Row 9**: Repeat row 5. Fasten off and leave long ends for sewing [22htr].

## FASCIA (D)

Ch 38 (You may have to adjust your stitch count to match your carboard piece.)

**Row 1**: 1 htr into third ch from hk (first 2 ch count as an htr); 1 htr into each ch across. Turn [37htr].

**Row 2**: Ch 2; 1 htr into each st across. Turn [37 htr].

**Rows 3—9**: Repeat row 2. Fasten off and leave long ends for sewing [37htr].

## PENDULUM DISCS (E)

Make 2 discs following the chart right, Make 1 purple for the back.
Make 1 using four colours for the front; row 1 pink, row 2 orange, row 3 red and row 4 purple (see Grafitti Door Pillow for written instructions).

## FACE (F)

In lilac, crochet a disc following the chart below, but for 6 rows in total.

## PENDULUM COVER (G)

Ch 28 (You may have to adjust your stitch count to match your piece of dowel.)

**Row 1**: 1 htr into third ch from hk (first 2 ch count as an htr); 1 htr into each ch across. Turn [27htr].

**Row 2**: Ch 2; 1 htr into each st across. Turn [27htr].

**Rows 3—4**: Repeat row 2. Fasten off and leave long ends for sewing [27htr].

## DOOR (H)

In lilac, ch 4. Join with sl st to form a ring.

**Row 1**: Ch 2 (counts as an htr here and

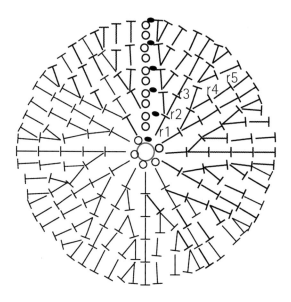

throughout); 7 htr into ring (do not join) (these 8 htr are the arch top of the door); ch 2; and turning work make 2 htr over the last htr made; 1 htr into beg 4ch ring; 2 htr over the first 2ch made at beg of this row; 1 htr into second ch of beg 2ch. Turn.

**Row 2**: (Making the rest of the door). Ch 2; 1 htr into each of the last 6 htr made. Turn [7htr].

**Row 3**: Repeat row 2. Fasten off. Weave in ends.

## OAK LEAF

Make 6. In green, ch 12.

**Row 1**: 1 dc into second ch from hk; 1 dc into next ch; 1 htr into next ch; 1 tr into each of next 4 ch; 1 dc into each of next 2 ch; 1 htr into next ch; 3 dc into last ch, rotating work and continuing on the other side of the ch working into the unused lps; 1 htr into next lp; 1 dc into next lp; 1 htr into the next lp; 1 tr into each of next 3 lps; 1 htr into next lp; 1 dc into each of next 3 lps; sl st into last lp; ch 1. Turn.

**Row 2**: 1 dc into next dc; 1 htr into next dc; 2 tr into next dc; sl st into next htr; 1 dc into next tr; 1 htr into next tr; 2 tr into next tr; 1 dc into next htr; 1 dc into next dc; sl st into next htr and into each of next 3 dc; 1 dc into next htr; 1 tr into next dc; sl st into next dc; 1 dc into next tr; 1 htr into next tr; 2 tr into next tr; sl st into next tr; 1 dc into next htr; 2 tr into next dc; 1 dc into next dc; sl st into first ch st from row 1. Fasten off. Weave in ends.

## CRAZY DAISY

Use the chart in the Crazy Daisy Lampshade to make 5 daisies with yellow for row 1 and lilac for row 2. Fasten off after each colour.

## GERBERA

Use the chart below to make 2 gerberas, one with a yellow centre and one with a lilac centre (row 1) and use red for row 2. Fasten off after each colour.

Gerbera (below)

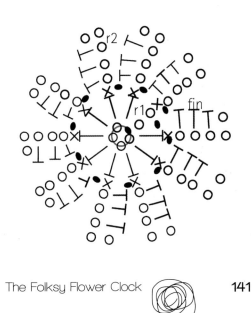

## LITTLE LEAF

Make 2 in orange following the chart in the Country Flower Cushion for written instructions.

## PURPLE FLOWER

Use the chart to make 3 flowers in purple.

## STAR FLOWER

Use the chart to make 1 Star Flower with yellow for row 1 and pink for row 2. Fasten off after each colour.

## ASSEMBLY

1    Make a hole in the centre of the main cardboard face where the hands of the clock will be fixed.

2    Centre the Face (E) on the Main Face (A) so that it lines up with the hole for the clock hands in the cardboard. Stitch neatly all around the edge.

3    Sew the Door on the Main Face (A) two rows above the Face (E). (Make sure the door does not interfere with the Fascia parts.)

4    Using a long doubled strand of blue

thread, make a large running stitch around the outer edge of the Main Face (A). Do not cut off.

5    Arrange the Main Face right side down on a work surface. Centre the cardboard template on top and paint glue around the edges. Gently pull up the running stitch so that it fits tightly over the edge of the cardboard. Hold in place with pegs or pins. Using the same blue thread lace across the back of the clock from side to side and; from the top to bottom to hold the crocheted face firmly in place. Avoid stitching over the area that the battery mechanism of the clock will occupy. Set aside to dry.

6    Fold Fascia Parts B, C, and D in half with wrong sides together. Sew neatly along one short edge and then along the long edge. Insert the cardboard pieces and sew the ends shut. Weave in the ends.

7    Repeat step 6 for Part G, inserting the dowel into the tube and attaching to the main body of the clock.

8    Cut a cardboard disc to fit just inside each Pendulum Disc (F) and sew neatly all

Purple flower (below) and Star Flower (right)

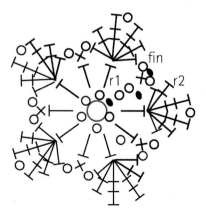

The Folksy Flower Clock

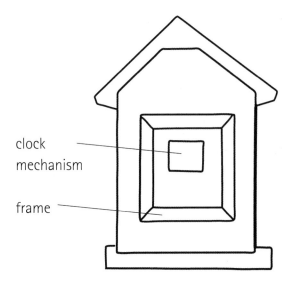

clock
mechanism

frame

**BACK VIEW**

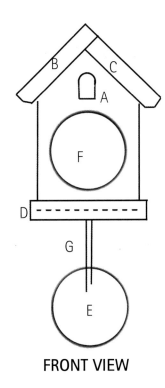

**FRONT VIEW**

the way around.

Stitch the dowel to the purple side of the disc positioning it one-third of the way up.

9 Glue the fascias to the Main Face allowing an overlap of 6 mm (¼ in) on all edges. Use pegs to hold in place, but be careful not to crush the cardboard.

10 Glue the clock mechanism in place in the centre of the clock.

11 Glue the photograph frame to the back of the clock. Tie the pendulum Post to the bottom of the photograph frame so that it swings freely. Allow to dry completely.

12 Glue the leaves and flowers in place.

## NATALIE'S NOTES

There is a folksy charm about the Cuckoo Clock. No doublt because they have been a part of our culture for centuries. Even in ancient times clocks were made with singing birds. My version is a simplistic take on the Swiss-chalet-style clock. I hope you enjoy making my modest interpretation of this popular and timeless classic.

The Folksy Flower Clock

# CRAZY DAISY LAMPSHADE

Embellish a lampshade with pretty motifs to give it a new lease of life. The pretty motifs are easy to make.

## MATERIALS

**Yarn**: Rico Essentials Cotton DK, 50 g (1¾ oz)

- 1 x col no 40 (Blue)
- 1 x col no 75 (Dark orange)
- 1 x col no 4 (Dark red)
- 1 x col no 2 (Red)
- 1 x col no 63 (Yellow)
- 1 x col no 69 (Pale orange)
- 1 x col no 68 (Salmon pink)

Lampshade

Quick-drying fabric adhesive

Dressmaking pins and/or clothes pegs

Wool sewing needle

Scissors

**Hook:** 3.5 mm

## TENSION

Tension is not important for this pattern.

## PATTERN

The number of motifs used on the lampshade in the photograph are given below. A larger or smaller lampshade will require different numbers. Make as many or as few of each as you like. Because this shade is so shapely I wanted the finished design to be simple with strong bold colours placed on the pale background.

## BRAID

Make 3 braids to fit around the top, middle and lower edge of the shade; using blue, dark orange and dark red.

Loosely make a ch until you have about 2 cm (3/4 in) more ch than will easily fit around the circumference of the shade.

**Next row**: Into third ch from hk, make 1 htr into each ch across. Once you get near the end, check you have made just enough to fit perfectly around the shade with a bit of stretch. Fasten off. Unravel the unused chains from the beginning sl st end, being careful not to unravel under your completed htrs.

Sew the last htr to the beg htr, weave in ends and glue in place. Hold securely using dressmaking pins and clothes pegs until the glue has dried.

## CRAZY DAISY

Make 2 in red and 2 in dark red, all with yellow centres, following the chart below.

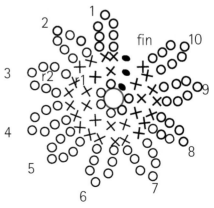

*Crazy Daisy Lampshade*

## LITTLE CIRCLE

Make 2 in pale orange, 4 in red and
4 in salmon pink.
Ch 4, join with sl st to form a ring.
**Row 1**: Ch 1; 10 dc into ring. Join with a sl st
to first dc. Fasten off [10dc].
Weave in ends and glue as desired upside
down so that the centres peak slightly.

## LITTLE LEAF

Make as many as required in pale orange.
This is the same motif as that used in the
Country Flower Cushion – see that project
for written instructions.

## MEDIUM LEAF

Make 5 in blue.
Ch 7; 1 dc into second ch from hk; 2 htr into
next ch; 2 tr into next ch; 2 htr into next ch,
1 dc into next ch; 3 dc into last ch, rotating
the work and working into the unused lps;
1 dc into next lp; 2 htr into next lp; 2 tr into
next lp; 2 htr into next lp; 1 dc into each of
the next 2 lps; sl st into first ch. Fasten off
Weave in ends and glue to lampshade
as desired.

can be purchased at charity shops. Look
for rust-free frames and fabric that is in
excellent condition. Remove any unwanted
braid or tassel trimmings carefully, then you
are ready to get creative.

## NATALIE'S NOTES

Upcycling is the new name for taking old,
secondhand or vintage items and giving
them a new lease of life. Old lampshades,

# CHRISTMAS SOCK

This is a softly shaped Christmas stocking reminiscent of yesteryear when people really did hang their socks and stockings up for Santa to fill. The pattern calls for a number of colour changes and a variety of textured stitches so it is the perfect project to test your crocheting skills.

**MATERIALS**
**Yarn**: Stylecraft Special DK, 100 g (3½ oz)
- 1 x Parchment, col no 1218 (Oatmeal)
- 1 x Pomegranate, col no 1083 (Pink)
- 1 x Raspberry, col no 1023 (Dark pink)
- 1 x Cloud blue, col no 1019 (Blue)
- 1 x White, col no 1001 (White)
- 1 x Cream, col no 1005 (Cream)
- 1 x Meadow, col no 1065 (Green)

Wool sewing needle
Scissors
**Hook**: 3.5 mm
**TENSION**
Tension is not important for this pattern.
**FINISHED SIZE**
52 cm (20½ in) from toe to folded-over cuff.

## SPECIAL PATTERN STITCHES

**Fptr = Front post treble**: Instead of making a tr into the st from the previous row, yo, insert hk around the whole of the post of the tr below, yo and pull through, yo and pull through 2 lps, yo and pull through remaining 2 lps on hk.

**Htr2tog = Half treble decrease**: Yo, insert hk into specified st, yo, pull through, yo and insert hk into next st, yo and pull through, yo and pull through all 5 lps on hk.

## PATTERN

For help with changing colour, see Techniques. The heel of the sock may be tricky to shape, so take your time.

In oatmeal, ch 11.

**Row 1**: 1 htr into third ch from hk, and into each ch across. Turn [10htr].

**Row 2**: Ch 2 (counts as an htr here and throughout this pattern); 1 htr into each htr across.

**Rows 3–22**: Repeat row 2.
Fasten off, leaving a long tail for sewing. Placing the short ends together, sew up the back seam, do not cut tail off as you will use this to gather the toe later.

**Row 23**: In pink, join at centre seam and make 2 dc into the side of the first htr. 1 dc into the next. Continue alternating 2 and 1 dcs around and end with 2 dc into the last side htr. Join with sl st to first dc, changing colour to bright pink [35dc].

**Row 24**: Ch 2; 1 htr into same sp as joining; 1 htr into each dc around. Join with sl st to second ch of beg 2ch. Change to blue [36htr].

**Row 25**: (Up-and-down stitch) Ch 3 (counts as a tr here and throughout); *1 dc into next st; 1 tr into next st. Repeat from * around. Join with sl st to third ch of beg 3ch.

**Row 26**: Ch 1 (does not count as a dc); 1 dc in same place as joining; *1 tr into next dc; 1 dc into next tr. Repeat from * around. Join with sl st to beg dc.

**Row 27**: Repeat row 25.

**Row 28**: Repeat row 26.

**Row 29**: Repeat row 25, changing to white when joining with the sl st. (5 rows of up-and-down-stitch).

**Row 30**: Ch 2; 1 htr into each st around. Join with sl st to second ch of beg 2ch. Change to cream [36htr].

**Row 31**: Ch 3; 1 tr into same sp as joining; 1 tr into each htr around. Join with sl st to third ch of beg 3ch [37tr].

**Row 32**: Ch 3; 1 tr into next tr, *1 fptr into next tr; 1 tr into next tr. Repeat from * around. Join with sl st to third ch of beg 3ch.

**Row 33**: Ch 1, 1 dc into same sp as joining; 1 dc into each of next 36 htr. Join with sl st to first dc. Fasten off [37 dc].

**Row 34**: With the back seam (joining stitches) at the back, count out 7 dcs to the left including the beg dc, and 7 dcs to the right, and place a stitch marker in each. (These two sts will be referred to as SM left and SM right. With the right side of the work facing you; join oatmeal in the SM right, ch 2 (counts as an htr); 1 htr into same sp as joining; 1 htr into each of the next 12 dcs; 2 htr into the next dc (SM left). Turn [16 htr]. Do not remove SM.

**Row 35**: Ch 1 (does not count as an htr); sk first htr; htr2tog over the next 2 htr; 1 htr in each of the next 11 htr; htr2tog over the next 2 htr. Turn [13htr].

**Row 36**: Ch 1; sk first htr; htr2tog over the next 2 htr; 1 htr in each of the next 8 htr, htr2tog over the next 2 htr. Turn [10htr].

**Row 37**: Ch 1; sk first htr; htr2tog over the next 2 htr; 1 htr into each of the next 5 htr; htr2tog over the next 2 htr. Turn. Fasten off [7htr].

**Row 38**: (Heel) Join with oatmeal into the SM right (from row 34); ch 2; 1 htr into same st as joining and into each st along the side of the rows 34–37 and into each htr across, and down the other side of the rows as before to the SM left st. Make 2 htrs into this st. Turn [18 htrs]. (If you find it difficult to place 18 sts add one to the centre or on the edges of row 37.)

**Row 39**: Ch1; sk first htr; htr2tog over next 2 htr; 1 htr into each of the next 13 htr; htr2tog over the next 2 htr. Turn [15htr].

**Row 40**: Ch1; sk first htr; htr2tog over next 2 htr; 1 htr into each of the next 10 htr; htr2tog over the next 2 htr. Turn [12htr].

**Row 41**: Ch1; sk first htr; htr2tog over next 2 htr; 1 htr into each of the next 7 htr; htr2tog over the next 2 htr. Turn. Fasten off [9htr].

**Row 42**: Join cream into centre st on heel. Ch 2; 1 htr into each st around over the oatmeal heel and into the unused sts from row 33. Join with sl st to first htr [46htr]. (As before, add an htr evenly if you find it difficult to get an exact number of sts.)

**Row 43**: Ch 2; (htr2tog over next 2 htr) twice; 1 htr into each of the next 2 htr; htr2tog over next 2 htr; 1 htr into each of the next 11 htr; htr2tog over next 2 htr; 1 htr into each of the next 2 htr; (htr2tog over next 2 htr) twice; 1 htr into each of the next 18 htr. Join with sl st to second ch of beg 2ch [40htr].

**Rows 44–45**: Following the chart below, and using pink and cream make the colour changes over the next two rows to the pattern using htrs for row 44 and dcs for row 45. Begin row 44 with a ch 2, and row 45 with (ch 1, dc into same st as joining). Join with a sl st at the end of each row.

**Row 46**: Ch1; 1 dc in same st as joining; 1 dc into each st across; join with sl st to first dc [40dc].

| 40 | 39 | 38 | 37 | 36 | 35 | 34 | 33 | 32 | 31 | 30 | 29 | 28 | 27 | 26 | 25 | 24 | 23 | 22 | 21 | 20 | 19 | 18 | 17 | 16 | 15 | 14 | 13 | 12 | 11 | 10 | 9 | 8 | 7 | 6 | 5 | 4 | 3 | 2 | 1 | |
|---|---|---|---|---|---|---|---|---|---|---|---|---|---|---|---|---|---|---|---|---|---|---|---|---|---|---|---|---|---|---|---|---|---|---|---|---|---|---|---|---|
| | | X | X | X | X | | | | X | X | X | X | | | | X | X | X | X | | | | X | X | X | X | | | | X | X | X | X | | | | | | | 45 |
| X | | | X | | | X | | | X | | | X | | | X | | | X | | | X | | | X | | | X | | | X | | | X | | | X | | | | 44 |

Row 47: Ch 2; (htr2tog over next 2 dc; 1 htr into each of the next 6 dc) 4 times; htr2tog over next 2 dc; 1 htr into each of the next 5 dc. Join with sl st to second ch of beg 2ch, changing colour to green [35htr].

Row 48: In green, repeat row 30, changing to cream [35htr].

Rows 49–50: In cream, repeat rows 31 and 32 [35htr].

Row 51: Continuing in cream, repeat row 30, changing to pink [35htr].

Row 52: In pink, repeat row 30, changing to white [35htr].

Row 53: In white, repeat row 30, changing to blue [35htr].

Row 54–60: In blue, repeat row 25 and row 26 three times, changing to white on the last row 25 repeat [35htr].

Row 61: In white, repeat row 30, changing to pink [35htr].

Row 62: In pink, repeat row 30, changing to dark pink [35htr].

Row 63: In dark pink, repeat row 30, changing to cream [35htr].

Rows 64–66: In cream, repeat row 30 [35 htr].

Rows 67–71: Following the chart below, and using pink and cream, make the colour changes over the next 5 rows of the pattern using htrs. Join with a sl st at the end of each row.

Rows 72–74: In cream, repeat row 30, changing to green [35htr].

Row 75: In green repeat row 30, changing to dark pink [35htr].

Row 76: In dark pink, repeat row 30, changing to pink [35htr].

Row 77: In pink, repeat row 30, changing to white [35htr].

Row 78: In dark pink, repeat row 30, changing to white [35htr].

Rows 79–84: In white, repeat row 30 [35htr].

Row 85: Ch 1, 2 dc in same st as joining; (2 dc in next dc, 1 dc into each of next 2 dc) 11 times; 1 dc into last dc. Join with sl st to first dc [47dc].

Rows 86–87: Continuing in white, repeat rows 31 and 32 [47tr].

Row 88: Continuing in white, repeat row 46, changing to pink [47dc].

Row 89: Ch 1; 1 dc in same sp as joining; 1 dc into next dc; * work (1 dc, ch 3, sl st into first ch [picot made], 1 dc) into next dc**; 1 dc in each of next 3 dc; repeat from * 11 times and from * to ** once. Fasten off.

| 35 | 34 | 33 | 32 | 31 | 30 | 29 | 28 | 27 | 26 | 25 | 24 | 23 | 22 | 21 | 20 | 19 | 18 | 17 | 16 | 15 | 14 | 13 | 12 | 11 | 10 | 9 | 8 | 7 | 6 | 5 | 4 | 3 | 2 | 1 | |
|---|---|---|---|---|---|---|---|---|---|---|---|---|---|---|---|---|---|---|---|---|---|---|---|---|---|---|---|---|---|---|---|---|---|---|---|
|  |  |  | X |  |  |  |  |  |  |  |  |  |  |  |  |  |  |  |  |  |  |  |  | X |  |  |  |  |  |  |  |  |  |  | 71 |
|  | X |  | X |  | X |  |  |  |  |  |  |  |  |  |  |  |  |  |  |  |  | X |  | X |  | X |  |  |  |  |  |  |  |  | 70 |
|  |  |  |  | X | X | X | X | X |  |  |  |  |  |  |  |  |  |  |  |  |  | X | X | X | X | X |  |  |  |  |  |  |  |  | 69 |
|  | X |  | X |  | X |  |  |  |  |  |  |  |  |  |  |  |  |  |  |  |  | X |  | X |  | X |  |  |  |  |  |  |  |  | 68 |
|  |  |  | X |  |  |  |  |  |  |  |  |  |  |  |  |  |  |  |  |  |  |  |  | X |  |  |  |  |  |  |  |  |  |  | 67 |

## ROPE

Make 1 short rope in white as a hanging lp, and 1 longer coloured rope to decorate the back of the stocking.

### For the Hanging Loop

In white, ch 23.

**Row 1**: In second ch from hk, 1 dc; 1 dc in each st across. Turn [22dc].

**Row 2**: Ch 1 (does not count as a dc); 1 dc into each st across. Turn [22dc].

**Row 3**: Ch 1; fold the two rows over bringing the first row forward so that the unused lp from the beg ch is in front of the lps of the second row, insert hk into the first unused lp of the beg ch and through the V-lps from the matching dc (from row 2), yo, pull through (sl st made); continue across to the end. Fasten off. Weave in ends. The result will be a
rounded rope.

### For the Coloured Rope Decoration

Follow the instructions for the Hanging Loop, but start with a ch length that measures 140 cm (55 in). (The exact number of ch is not important.) Begin with pink, and complete row 1, changing to green for row 2. Work the sl st (row 3) in white. Fasten off. Weave in ends and tie into a large bow.

## FINISHING

Turn over top edge on row 85 to form a cuff. Stitch through both layers in white all the way around. Do not cut the thread.

Fold over Hanging Loop and push through from under the cuff so that it emerges at the top of the cuff. Sew in place firmly. Attach Coloured Rope on the outside of the cuff exactly behind the Hanging Loop ensuring that the bow is attractively arranged.

## NATALIE'S NOTES

The Christmas stocking was often hung in front of the fireplace and sometimes on bedposts. I have designed this stocking to look like a sock so it has a soft drape. Try out your own colour variations to match your choice of Christmas décor.

# SNOWFLAKE HANGING

Make these elegant little snowflakes to decorate the Christmas tree or to make a fabulous window hanging. Add beads to some to give them a little sparkle. This project is a great introduction to thread crochet.

## MATERIALS
**Yarn**: Coats & Clark Aida, 50 g (1¾ oz)
- Size 5, col no 00001 (white)
- Size 10, col no 0001 (white)
- Size 15, col no 0001 (white)

Large-eye sewing needle
Scissors
Glass beads

**Hooks**: These are recommended sizes, but find the hook size that suits your tension. The smaller the hook the tighter the snowflake.
- 1.75–2 mm for size 5 thread
- 1.5–1.75 mm for size 10 thread
- 1.25–1.5 mm for size 15 thread

## TENSION
Tension is not important. However, it is important to keep the snowflake flat. Too tight a tension and the snowflake will curl, too loose and it will droop.

## FINISHED SIZE
Variable depending on the thickness of the thread.

## SPECIAL PATTERN STITCHES

**Ch2 picot = Chain 2 picot**: Make ch 2 and then sl st into second ch from hk (picot made).

**Beg spcl = Beginning split cluster**: Ch 4, make 1 dtr into same dc as joining, leaving the last lp of the st on hk; make 2 dtr into next dc, leaving the last lps of each dtr on hk; yo and pull through all 4 lps on hk.

**Split cl = Split cluster**: Into each of the next 2 dc make 2 dtrs, leaving the last lp of each dtr on the hk; yo and pull through all 5 lps on the hk.

**Trcl = Treble cluster**: Make 3 trs into the sp, but leave the last lp of each st on the hk, yo and pull through all 4 lps on the hk.

**Dtrcl = Double treble cluster**: Make 4 dtrs into the sp, but leave the last lp of each st on the hk, yo and pull through all 5 lps on the hk.

## INSERTING BEADS

Insert the glass beads when you see (B). See Techniques for more information.

**Note** that you should insert the bead onto the live part of the thread before making the picot in row 2.

## PATTERN

Three thicknesses of thread have been used to make the snowflakes pictured in this project. The instructions are the same for each thread size. This pattern uses a lot of clusters to shape the snowflake. They are easy to make.

Thread the beads onto the crochet thread before you start; 24 beads are required for each one, but string a few extra on just to be sure there are enough.

Ch6. Join with sl st to form a ring.

**Row 1**: Ch 4 (counts as a dtr here and throughout), into ring work: 1 dtr; ch 3; (2 dtr, ch 3) 5 times. Join with sl st to fourth ch of beg 4ch [6 3ch sps].

**Row 2**: Ch 1, 1 dc into same place as joining; 1 dc into next dtr; *(1 dc, 1 htr, ch 2 picot (B), 1 htr, 1 dc) into 3ch lp. 1 dc in each of next 2 dtrs. Rep from * 4 times. (1 dc, 1 htr, ch 2 picot, 1 htr, 1 dc) into next 3ch lp. Join with sl st into first dc.

**Row 3**: Beg spcl; (ch 12, spcl) 5 times; ch 12. Join with sl st to top of beg spcl.

**Row 4**: Sl st into 12ch sp; ch 1; into this and each of the next 5 12ch sps work the following: (2 dc, ch 2 (B), 1 trcl, ch 3, dtrcl, ch 5, dtrcl, ch 3, trcl, ch 2 (B), 2 dc). Join with sl st to first dc.

**Row 5**: Rev sl st into sp between the first and last dcs worked in row 4. Ch1, dc in same sp; (*ch 5, 1 dc into next 3ch sp; ch 5; 1 dc into next 5ch sp, ch 3, 1 dc into the same 5ch sp; ch 5; 1 dc into the next 3ch sp; ch 5**; sk next 2 dcs; make 1 dc between 2 dc) 5 times. Repeat from * to ** once. Join with sl st into first dc.

**Row 6**: Sl st into next 5ch sp; *into each of the next 2 5ch sps work (2 dc, 1 htr, 2 dc); (2 tr, 1 dtr (B), 2tr) into next 3ch sp; work (2 dc, 1 htr, 2 dc) into each of the next 2 5ch sps. Rep from * 5 more times. Join with sl st to first dc. Fasten off. Weave in ends.

## BLOCKING AND STIFFENING

The snowflakes should be stretch-blocked and can also be steamed, but be careful not to melt the plastic beads, if you have used them. Pull the snowflakes out to reach their maximum stretch. See Techniques.

## TO MAKE A HANGING

You will need three varying lengths of dowel. Drill a hole in the centre of each dowel and string together, placing a large bead between the dowels. Tie lengths of fine white satin ribbon along the dowels and then tie the ribbon to the snowflakes.

## VARIATION

It is possible to make a table runner or a centrepiece cloth by joining several motifs. Join two points using the join-as-you-go method in the last row of the pattern.

# GINGERBREAD HOUSE

Perfect as a Christmas or children's party table decoration, or for hanging from a tree, this sweet little gingerbread house is sure to become a family treasure.

## MATERIALS
**Yarn**: Rowan Cotton Glace, 50 g (1¾ oz)
- 1 x Toffee, col no 843 (Gingerbread)

Small amounts of
- Bleached, col no 726 (White)
- Poppy, col no 741 (Red)
- Garnet, col no 841 (Lilac)
- Ivy, col no 812 (Dark green)
- Bubbles, col no 724 (Pink)
- Shoot, col no 814 (Light green)
- Persimmon, col no 832 (Orange)

Wool sewing needle

Pen

Cardboard

Scissors

Cellotape or masking tape

Quick-drying fabric adhesive

**Hook**: 3.25 mm

## TENSION
20 dc and 24 rows will make a piece 9 cm (3½ in) wide.

## FINISHED SIZE
9 x 8 x 7 cm (3½ x 3¼ x 2¾ in).

## SPECIAL PATTERN STITCHES

**Spike sl st = Spike slip stitch**: A spike st reaches down into the row below. Insert hk into the sp specified, yo, pull through and continue to pull through lp on hk.

**Dc2tog = Double crochet decrease**: Insert hk into specified st, yo and draw through, insert hk into next st, yo and draw through, yo and draw through all 3 lps on hk. (Decrease made).

## PATTERN

The pattern for the inner cardboard structure is below. Make this first, so you can test fit your pieces. Make the first piece, test the fit, and adjust your tension accordingly. All of the gingerbread house is made in a dc st so if necessary change the st counts or reduce/increase your hk size.

## ASSEMBLING THE BOX

Draw the pattern onto medium-weight cardboard. Lightly score the foldlines and fold into place. Use cellotape or masking tape to seal the edges of the structure together.

## MAKING THE 'GINGERBREAD'

Made 2 roof pieces, 2 sides, 1 base, 1 back and 1 front. The sides and the base are the same size. Follow the Basic Pattern for instructions and the table below, which sets out the number of rows and sts for each part. See the insructions for Shaping the Front and Back pieces

## TABLE OF PARTS ROWS AND STITCHES

| Section | Ch | No of dc | No of rows |
|---|---|---|---|
| Roof | 21 | 20 | 24 |
| Sides/Base | 18 | 17 | 36 |
| Front/Back | 14 | 13 | 12* |

* Do not fasten off. See instruction for shaping front and back.

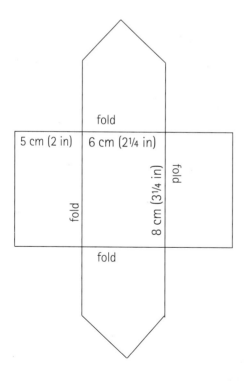

5 cm (2 in)　6 cm (2¼ in)

8 cm (3¼ in)

fold

fold

fold

fold

fold

Gingerbread House

## BASIC PATTERN

With gingerbread yarn, make the number of sts specified in the table below:

**Row 1**: Into second ch from hk, dc; 1 dc into each st across. Turn. (The number of dcs will be one less than the beg ch.)

**Row 2**: Ch 1 (does not count as a dc here and throughout); 1 dc into each st across. Complete as many rows as specified in the table, fasten off and weave in the ends.

## SHAPING FOR THE FRONT AND BACK

**Rows 1–12** as Basic Pattern.

**Row 13**: Ch 1; sk 1 dc; 1 dc in each of next 9 dc; dc2tog at the end [11dc].

**Row 14**: Ch 1; sk 1 dc; 1 dc in each of next 7 dc; dc2tog at the end [9dc].

**Row 15**: Ch 1; sk 1 dc; 1 dc in each of next 5 dc; dc2tog at the end [7dc].

**Row 16**: Ch 1; sk 1 dc; 1 dc in each of next 3 dc; dc2tog at the end [5dc].

**Row 17**: Ch 1; sk 1 dc; 1 dc in next dc; dc2tog at the end [3dc].

**Row 18**: Ch 1; dc3tog. Fasten off. Weave in ends.

## SNOW RIDGE

Make 2. In white, ch 19.

**Row 1**: Dc into second ch from hk; 1 dc into each st across. Turn [18dc].

**Row 2**: Ch 2; 1 tr, 1 htr into 1st dc; *sl st into next dc; 1 dc into next dc; sl st into next dc; (1 htr, 1 tr, 1htr (shell made)) into next dc; repeat from * three more times; sl st into last dc. Fasten off.

With wrong sides facing, dc the ridge pieces together using the unused lps from the beg ch.

## ROOF EDGING

In white, ch 62.

Follow the instructions for the Snow Ridge, row 1 will have 61 dc and fits in one piece all around the roof edge.

Repeat the pattern 21 times in total plus the beg shell (22 shells).

(Test the length of ch to make sure it goes around the card structure, allowing a bit of a stretch; if necessary add 1 or 2 ch and sl st into these on the corners. The beginning ch is a unit of 4 plus 2.)

## CANDY CANES

In white, ch 11.

**Row 1**: Dc into second ch from hk; 1 dc into each st across. Turn [5 dc].

**Rows 2–4**: Ch 1 (does not count as a dc here and throughout); 1 dc into each st across.

**Row 5**: Fold the cane over, and sl st the last row to the unused lps from the beg ch.

With red, sew at an angle around the rope.

## DOOR

In lilac, ch 6.

**Row 1**: Dc into second ch from hk; 1 dc into each st across. Turn [5 dc].

**Rows 2–6**: Ch 1 (does not count as a dc here and throughout); 1 dc into each st across.

**Row 7**: Ch 1; sk first dc, 1 dc into each of next 3 dc; sl st into last dc. Fasten off.
In red, top sl st all around the door. Weave in ends.

## WREATH

In dark green, ch 7. Join with sl st to form a ring.

**Row 1**: Ch 2 (counts as an htr); 13 htr into ring. Join with sl st to second ch of beg 2ch [14 htr].

**Row 2**: (Ch 2; sl st into first ch (picot made); sl st into next htr) 7 times. Join with sl st to base of beg 2ch. Fasten off. Weave in ends. Thread red yarn through a lp on the first row and tie a little bow. Apply a small amount of adhesive to the knot to stick in place.

## ROUND CANDIES (On roof top)

Make 5 in total; 2 red, 1 pink, 1 light green and 1 orange.

**Row 1**: Ch 2; 4 dc into second ch from hk. Fasten off. Sew closed catching the 4 dc in a running stitch to make a tight ball. Weave in ends.

## LITTLE CANDIES

Make 15 in total; 6 light green, 3 red, 3 orange and 3 pink.

**Row 1**: Ch 2; 8 dc into second ch from hk. Join with sl st to beg 2ch. Fasten off. Weave in ends.

## LARGE RED-AND-WHITE CANDIES

Make 5.

**Row 1**: In white ch 2; 8 dc into second ch from hk. Join with sl st to beg 2ch [8dc].

**Row 2**: Ch 3; 1 tr into same st as joining; 2 tr into each dc [16tr]. Fasten off.

**Row 3**: With red, join into any tr; sl st into next tr; *spike sl st into the base of the next tr (in the hole made where the 2 trs were worked into the dc from row 1); sl st into next 2 trs; repeat from * 6 times; spike sl st into next st. Join with sl st to first sl st. Fasten off. Weave in ends.

## ASSEMBLY

1   Glue the gingerbread pieces onto the cardboard, making sure that the glue adheres to the cellotape on each corner. Allow to dry thoroughly before adding the smaller motifs.

2   Glue the snow ridge to the apex of the roof.

3   Glue the roof edging in place starting in a corner and allowing the centre shells to overlap slightly. (There should be 5 shells down the length of the roof and 3 shells on each front and back roof apex.)

4   Glue the candy canes to each corner so that they cover the edges.

5   Choose the front of the house, and carefully position the door, wreath and two green little candies. Glue in place.

6   Glue the round candies onto the roof.

7   Glue 4 of the large red-and-white candies to the roof, two on each side.

**8** Glue 1 large red-and-white candy to the back, and three little candies below it.

**9** Glue the remaining little candies to the sides.

## VARIATION

You could get very creative and make these little gingerbread houses into gift boxes by making the lid removable and lining the insides of the box. They also make great table decorations or placeholders.

# USEFUL INFORMATION

# Techniques

Every experienced crocheter has their own repertoire of tips and tricks to make their stitches neat and even. Find your own way of working — it doesn't make your method wrong. Explore other maker's tips, test to see what works for you. Most of all try to understand crochet. Understand how a stitch is built, how a fabric is made and how an item is created.

## TENSION

Getting the tension correct is often a concern, especially for beginners. If it is difficult to push the hook through the work, then your tension is too tight; change to a bigger hook size, even a tiny adjustment can make a big difference. Alternatively, try to relax your hands and the flow of thread over your little finger. Crocheting too tightly may hurt your hands and your work may distort.

When you are crocheting, your rhythm should be easy, flowing and relaxed. The stitches will be mostly even and regular in size. If you have been working for a while on fine thread, for example, and then change to chunky wool, it may take some time for your tension to adjust.

Tension is not important for some of the projects in this book. However, if there is a tension guide, it is advisable to make a tension swatch. Crochet a small piece of the work about 10 cm (4 in) square and measure it. Check how it compares to the tension guide given. Change to a larger hook if the swatch is too small and try again. If the swatch is too big, use a smaller hook.

## PREPARING YOUR YARN

Usually yarn and thread are sold in balls. Some makers prefer to work with the thread from the inside of the ball, some from the outside. Whatever your preferred method, make sure you complete the project using all the yarn in the same direction. As you crochet you may find it easier to unwind some yarn instead of working off the ball as this can create annoying and unnecessary tension. Pull the yarn from the ball allowing it to pile up on your right-hand side, then, pull the unwound yarn back across to your left side. Make sure that there is nothing to prevent the yarn flowing freely to your hook.

If you bought yarn in skeins, see Natalie's Notes for the Hot Heart Cosy to prepare skeins prior to working.

Thread tends to unravel from its cone much more easily than wool, so place the cone in a plastic bag, tied loosely closed, so that the thread stays clean, but is free to bounce around while you work.

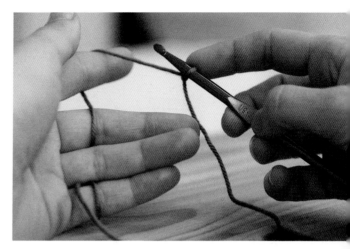

## HOLDING THE YARN

In the photo above you will see that the yarn is held in the left hand and is wound over the small finger to help control the flow of the yarn. It then passes over the forefinger—to help control the tension. By lifting your forefinger you control the feed of yarn to the hook, which will affect your tension.

## HOLDING THE HOOK

There are two main ways to hold the hook, either like a pen or like a knife. On standard metal hooks there is often a flat section for you to grip. Handmade wooden hooks don't always have this. Hold the hook with either face toward you or downwards.

Essentially, the chin of the hook does not rotate when you work, instead it is the wrist that swivels so that the hook moves backwards and forwards, and up and down, but doesn't twist. If you like to hold your hook with the chin facing downward then that is how it should remain while you stitch. Practise working rows of stitches keeping the chin of the hook facing in one direction until it feels natural. You will soon build a rhythm.

# Stitches

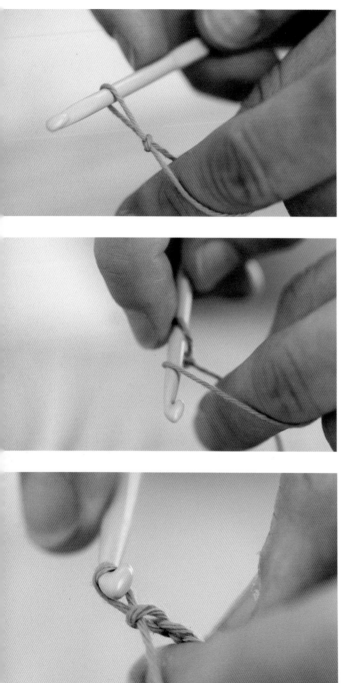

## SLIP KNOT

The standard method to start crochet is to make a slip knot to make your working loop. This never counts as a stitch and should not be confused with a slip stitch.

## CHAIN STITCH (CH)

To make a chain stitch, pass the hook around the yarn and pull through the working loop already on the hook. The completed chain stitches are V-shaped. Often this V-shape is referred to in patterns.

---

**Tip** Learn to recognise stitches both from the front and from behind. For instance when working, a right-handed crocheter will have the V part of stitch to the right of the stem (post) of the main stitch. When working into this stitch on subsequent rows your hook needs to pass perfectly under both loops of this V. It is important that you can learn to 'see' this V. Remember that when you turn the work at the end of a row the V will be on the left side of the stem (post) of the stitch.

Sometimes the pattern will ask you to work into the front loop or the back loop of a stitch. The front loop refers to the loop of the V closest to you, and the back loop the one at the back.

---

## FOUNDATION CHAIN

At the beginning of a flat piece of crochet you will be asked to crochet a number of chain stitches. These should usually be made looser or made with a larger size of hook. In the next row work into the bottom loop of the V-stitch so that the rest of the chain stitch becomes enveloped into the new stitch, leaving just a loop visible. (These loops are referred to as the unused loops.)

## TURNING CHAINS (BEGINNING CHAINS)

At the beginning of each row, you will need to build up a number of chain stitches for the next row so that they may act as a substitutes for another type of stitch. Normally 4ch substitutes for a double treble, 3ch equals a treble, 2ch a half treble and sometimes a 1ch equals a double crochet although there are exceptions:

• In this book, 2ch is often, but not always used instead of 3ch to substitute a treble. I have found it to be a neater substitute length than what is considered standard practise, but you need to find your own method and choose what looks right for the particular project depending on hook size and yarn used.

• A single chain stitch is commonly used to build height at the beginning of a row for a double crochet. However, in this book, it is rarely used as a substitute for the double crochet stitch. I get a more professional result to make the following stitches at the

beginning of a row: ch 1, 1 dc in same sp...... (cont). At the end of that row, you will need to join to the first double crochet and not the first chain stitch or you will be creating an additional stitch.

At the end of a row, turn, and then work the turning chain. It allows for a neater edge. Then skip the first stitch and work the first pattern stitch into the next stitch.

## SLIP STITCH (SL ST)

(Below) This is really the same stitch as a chain stitch, but it is applied in a 3 different ways:

### Joining Stitch

Usually at the end of a round, it is necessary to join the last stitch to the first stitch of the same round. To do this, insert the hook into the gap below the V part of the stitch, yarn over hook and pull through the working loop on the hook. This creates a sideways chain stitch over the work already done without creating an actual working stitch. If you are

joining into a chain stitch insert the hook in the left side of the chain stitch V.

## Re-positioning

A pattern will often call for you to reposition the starting place and the pattern will ask you to sl st into the stitch ahead and sometimes in reverse. The stitch is made in exactly the same way as described for the Joining Stitch.

## Top Stitch

At times a slip stitch is used to Top Stitch. This is where a loop is made (not a slip knot) and pulled to the front of the work into an indicated position. The ball of yarn is left under the work; insert the hook, yarn over hook and pull through beginning loop. Continue as instructed. This kind of stitch forms a pretty surface stitch in the shape of a V and is used for definition, usually in a contrasting colour.

## Reverse Slip Stitch (rev sl st)

This is used after joining at the end of a row. Insert the hook into the last stitch completed before joining, yarn over and pull through.

## JOINING TO FORM A RING

(Below left) Many patterns in this book ask you to make a number of chain and then to join with a slip stitch to form a ring. In the next round you will almost always be asked to work a number of stitches into that ring to form the basis of the rest of the pattern. When you join with the sl st to the first ch, join into the bottom part of the V. This will prevent the stitch from opening up.

## DOUBLE CROCHET FOUNDATION CHAIN (DC FC)

This stitch is used to make a braid or to start a piece of crochet without using a foundation chain especially where a lot of stitches are required and it becomes difficult to get an accurate count.

Start with a slip knot, ch 2, into second ch from hook, dc, ch 1, dc into side of previous dc, ch 1. Continue until you have reached the desired length.

## HALF TREBLE CROCHET (HTR)

(Below) Yarn over hook, insert hook in stitch indicated, yarn over and pull through, yarn over and pull through all three loops on hook.

This stitch is known as half double crochet (hdc) in US crochet terminology.

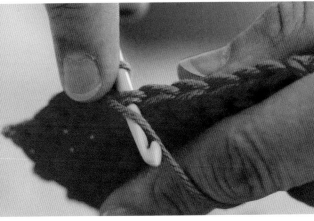

## DOUBLE CROCHET (DC)

(Above) Insert hook in stitch, yarn over and pull through, yarn over and pull through both loops on the hook. This stitch is known as single crochet (sc) in US crochet terminology.

## TREBLE CROCHET (TR)

(Below) Yarn over hook, insert hook in stitch indicated, yarn over and pull through (there are now 3 loops on hook), yarn over and pull through two loops, yarn over and pull through remaining two loops on hook.

This stitch is known as double crochet (dc) in US crochet terminology.

## DOUBLE TREBLE CROCHET

(Above) Yarn over hook twice, insert hook in stitch indicated, yarn over and pull through (there are now 4 loops on hook), yarn over and pull through two loops, yarn over and pull through two loops, yarn over and pull through remaining two loops on hook.

This stitch is known as a treble crochet (tr) in US crochet terminology.

## TREBLE TREBLE STITCH

(Below) Yarn over hook three times, insert hook in stitch indicated, yarn over and pull through, (there are now 5 loops on hook) yarn over and pull through two loops, yarn over and pull through two loops, yarn over and pull through two loops, yarn over and pull through remaining two loops on hook.

This stitch is known as a double treble crochet (dtr) in US crochet terminology.

## SPIKE STITCH

Occasionally a pattern will ask you to make a stitch in a row further back in the work where you are. Proceed to make the type of stitch as indicated by the pattern in the normal way and then continue working in the current row. This type of stitch will tend to pull the work into a certain shape.

## CLUSTERS

Clusters are made by working a number of stitches in a grouping. Each pattern will tell you how to create the cluster for that particular part of the pattern. Normally the stitch is worked part of the way leaving the last loop of each stitch on the hook together with the beginning loop.

# Other Techniques

## UNDERSTANDING THE PATTERN

Always read the pattern notes and at least skim read through the rest of the pattern. Check to see that you understand any Special Pattern stitches. Repeated instructions normally cause the most confusion and you should read the section The Basics at the beginning of the book that explains how repeat instructions are given.

## INCREASING AND DECREASING

Some of the patterns will ask you to increase and decrease stitches; for example htr2dec. This means that you need to make a decrease stitch over the next two half treble stitches.

Increasing and decreasing are both used to shape an item and may happen anywhere

in a row. To increase the work, you will be asked to do more than one stitch into the stitch from the previous row.

And accordingly, to decrease, you will be asked to crochet two or more stitches together. Work the stitch as normal into the first of the stitches specified until there is only one stage to the stitch construction left, start working on the next stitch in the same way, and then join the two stitches together by yarn over and pulling through all the loops remaining on the hook The pattern notes will then count the stitch as one, because only one V-stitch remains.

## CROCHET BETWEEN STITCHES

Sometimes a pattern will ask you to crochet between the stitches. This means to work between the posts of the stitch and not through the top V part.

## JOINING NEW YARN OR CHANGING COLOUR

At times it is necessary to join a new ball of yarn to the existing work, It should be joined in the same manner as changing colour – and that is part-way through a stitch – on the last stroke. So if you are making a htr (half treble) yarn over, insert hook, pull through, with new yarn, yarn over and pull through all three loops on hook. Do not knot the ends together, and weave in the ends in the usual way, being careful not to pull it too tight.

If you are Joining in to a piece of work that has been fastened off, simply insert hook and pull through a loop, then yarn over and pull through. (This is called joining with a slip stitch.) Continue working the pattern and remember to leave a long enough tail to weave in securely when you have finished the work.

## WEAVING IN ENDS

This is the part all crocheters dislike. But done properly will ensure that your creation stays looking good for years.

Whenever you start a piece of crochet it is advisable to work over the beginning end, unless the pattern tells you not to. However this is not sufficient to secure the ends and you should still weave the end in a little bit more.

Using a yarn needle sew the tail ends into the fabric of the piece weaving in between and through stitches on the back of the work in such a way that it is not noticeable.

For very lacy work and thread crochet it is better to closely match the actual stitches by almost recreating it. Using your needle and thread, try to match the path of the crocheted stitch by weaving in and out. For yarn it is advisable to weave about 10 cm (4 in) of yarn, for thread crochet about 5 cm (2 in) is more than sufficient.

For acrylic yarns it is more difficult to

weave in yarn ends successfully as they have a tendency to slide out. Some makers advise tying knots in the ends, but this is not a pretty method. The best way to weave in with acrylic is to work back, forward, up and down. It is also advisable to split threads at some points, pushing the needle through the yarn.

Always check the tension as you weave in so that you do not distort the piece.

## JOINING MOTIFS

There are three main ways to do this. The motif based patterns in this book mostly use the join-as-you-go method. But it is also possible to crochet them together or to sew them together.

### Join-as-you-go

There are a number of ways you can use the Join-as-you-go method of joining motifs. The motifs are joined in the last round of crocheting by substituting a chain stitch with a dc in the corresponding stitch of the other motif. The patterns all give explicit instructions where to join each motif. Place the completed motif behind the motif you are working on so the wrong sides are together, insert hook into space or stitch (as indicated in the pattern) of the completed motif, yarn over, pull through, yarn over and pull through both loops on hook. Continue to work on the new motif until you get to the next joining place.

### Double Crochet Together

Place the wrong sides of the work together, carefully matching the stitches up and using wool pins to hold the work in place. Join with the required colour—preferably in a corner and then dc through both layers checking often to see that your work is neat and consistent on the back piece. This method will leave a raised rib of dc along the right side of the work and is perfect for cushion covers as it leaves a neat edge.

### Sewing Together

Arrange the two pieces to be joined side by side with right sides of the work down. Pin in place so that the pieces align. Fasten your yarn by making a carefully placed double stitch in the first crochet stitch.

If you are sewing the tops parts of the stitch together sew in a zig zag from one side to the other going around and under each V stitch. If you are sewing the sides of rows together then stitch round the top and the bottom of the stitches. Keep the stitches firm, but do not pull too tightly or the fabric will pucker up. End off the seam with a double stitch to secure the yarn. Weave in the tail end.

### Backstitching

To create a secure seam, and one where the seam edges are raised at the front or back of the work. Place the two parts to be joined right sides together where you want the seam to be behind the work; or wrong sides together where you want seam to be raised and visible. Pin in place. Secure the yarn; skip the first stitch; and then working under the Vs pass the needle under and back through the missed V of the previous stitch; skip the stitch just worked; and the next stitch and pass the needle through again as before. Continue in this way.

### BLOCKING

To obtain a lovely finish of your work it is useful to block the item. Not all items made need to be blocked—it will depend on the yarn used. Thread crochet items are always blocked to stretch the crochet out so that the pattern is noticeable. Acrylic items rarely require blocking unless it is a heavily topstitch and dense piece. It is standard practise to block items like shawls and in this book instructions are given where it is deemed necessary to block an item. But if you have substituted the yarn then you will have to use your own judgement.

Lay the item out—use a spare bed or a carpeted floor. For small items it is possible to use the ironing board. Using blocking pins, pull and shape the item until it is stretched. Spray with a fine mist of water. Allow to dry and leave to rest for a few days.

## Steam blocking

Follow the same method as above but use a steam iron or a steamer instead of the water mist. Allow the iron to hover above the crochet and avoid touching it. It is advisable to cover the crochet with a press cloth to catch any drops of water. Avoid using this method for acrylic-based items.

## STARCHING

For thread crochet, rinse the item. It will tend to pucker up. Flatten it out and stretch to shape using pins. Steam block and allow to dry. Spray with starch evenly. You may want several applications of starch until you have the desired rigidity of stiffness. You can also steam iron the item between starch applications to speed up the drying time, but use a press cloth to prevent damage to the crochet.

If a proprietary spray starch is not stiff enough, then use laundry starch that comes in a powder form and mix according to their directions.

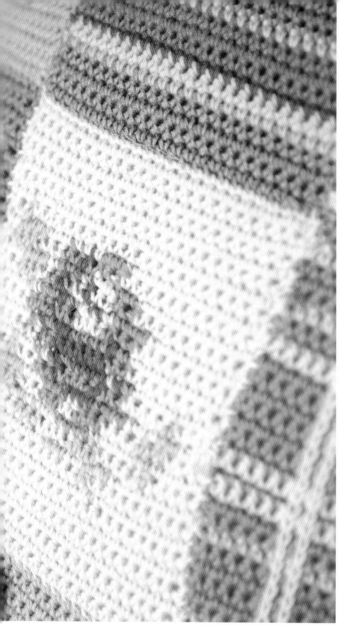

A benefit of starching doilies is that it keeps them lying flat and resistant to dirt.

## Natalie's Homemade Starch

It is also possible to starch an item using cornflour (cornstarch) and water. Mix a teaspoon of cornflour (cornstartch) with a cup of hot water that has just come off the boil. Mix until it becomes opaque and jelly-like. Immerse the item of crochet into the mixture and block as before. The starch can be stored in a glass jar in the refrigerator for a while, and can also be made much stronger by simply increasing the ratio of cornstarch to water.

### A Note of Caution

There are proprietary products for the stiffening of crochet and other fabrics. These products contain glues—normally PVA-based—but think about it very carefully. Starch washes out, but glues never do. There is also a tendency for the glues to cause the crochet to become yellowed with age.

### STUFFING

Some of the projects require that you stuff them. Some of the stuffing is made from recycled materials—the best being old (clean) t-shirts and women's tights. The material is flexible and allows you to stuff items easily and for domestic items are a good alternative to synthetic stuffing and much easier to use and ecologically friendly.

Cut the material into thin strips about 1 cm ($1/3$ in). Stuff the item firmly but do not overstuff. Use your fingers to manipulate the stuffing so that it is distributed evenly. You may find it helpful to use a large knitting needle and/or a crochet hook to help push the stuffing into place.

If you are stuffing toys then it is advisable to stuff the item much more firmly as the article is handled much more than the decorative items in this book.

## USING BEADS

It is fun to use beads in crochet. There are a couple of important tips to remember.

• The beads show more clearly on the wrong side of the work, so consider the pattern and the final use of the item for any application of beads.

• Use beads that will not melt—so glass and wooden beads are ideal.

• Thread the beads onto the yarn or crochet thread before starting work. Count carefully, but always add a few more beads than necessary.

• Always choose beads where the hole is reasonably suitable for the size of the yarn—a tiny glass bead will not work with a Double Knit yarn.

### How to Thread Beads onto Thicker Yarn

Even suitable beads may have very small holes and it may be impossible to thread straight onto the yarn. Thread a beading needle with a fine piece of sewing thread about 20 cm (8 in) long and knot the two ends tightly so there is almost no bump. Thread the thicker yarn through this thread loop, thread the beads onto the needle, pass down the sewing thread and onto the folded over yarn. Push down until the bead is securely on the main yarn. Continue until all your beads are loaded.

## MAKING A POM POM

A pop pom is a ball made of cut ends of thread. You can buy pom pom makers, but it is possible to make your own.

You need two circles from cardboard, cut to the size you want your pom pom to be. Cut an inner circle out—the closer your inner circle is to the outer the fuller and more dense your pom pom will be. Using another piece of card—about 10 cm (4 in) long and about 5 mm (¼ in) wide, wind a length of yarn around it. This is your shuttle. Place the two circles together and holding it in your left hand begin to pass the shuttle of yarn through the centre of the circles and wrap it over the cardboard circles as evenly as possible. You will need to reload the shuttle from time to time until it becomes impossible to pass the shuttle through the centre. Then use a yarn needle and a long length of yarn and continue in the same way.

Once the circles are completely covered and it is not possible to add anymore yarn, you cut through the yarn on the outside of the circles using a very sharp pair of scissors, Cut through the yarn and between the two circles. Pull the two circles away from each other, but do not remove entirely. Wrap a doubled length of yarn around the middle of the pom pom—between the two circles—and tie securely. If you are going to stitch the pom pom to anything then leave these lengths to use for sewing. Fluff and trim your pom pom carefully so that it looks even and rounded.

Remember that if you are making more than one pompom for a project, try to make them all the same size—so keep the fullness on the circles the same. The more tightly you wrap, the fuller your pom pom will be.

## FELTING

Wash the crocheted item in a 40%–60% machine wash using only detergent. (Please read the yarn manufacturers guidance as to the temperature—if you are not sure start at the lower temperature and repeat the process.)

It is useful to put a pair of old jeans into the machine as it helps to agitate the wool and will aid with the shrinking. When the cycle is finished take the item out and lay on a towel. Gently pull to shape it, stretching and tugging until the items looks right. Leave for a day or two to dry in a cool, well-ventilated room. (Please don't dry with heat.)

## CARING FOR CROCHET

Always follow the manufacturer's instructions when caring for crochet. As a rule of thumb, wash by hand or on the most delicate of cycles at low heat. Acrylic-based items are more robust, but nevertheless avoid washing them with other heavier items in the machine. Always dry flat and block if required.

Store all crochet away from heat and damp. If you have to fold an item for a long period of time it is advisable to refold the piece to allow the fibres to relax on the old foldlines. Fabrics should be stored with suitable moth prevention.

Never store an item with old linen that has a musty smell as that will spread and cause damage to your lovely work.

## TROUBLESHOOTING

Before you panic always check the pattern and read the instructions again.

Some of the common problems are:

**Work Wont Lie Flat**: Your tension is too tight, the hook too small, or perhaps it is the way the pattern is written and it may pull out further in the pattern.

**Distortion or Twist:** There is always some twist to crochet, especially if you are working in the round. If you are right-handed the twist will be to the right and vice versa for left-handed people. The twist is often seen in very open lacy patterns done in the round where the centre seems to be tighter than the surround. This is normal and can be overcome by changing to a smaller hook once you have reached the point where the distortion becomes noticeable.

**Running Out of Yarn:** Reserving a few extra balls of yarn is always a good idea at the time you purchase and most good suppliers will allow you to do this. You can also try to find if anyone on www.ravelry.com has any in their stash. Always keep the yarn labels to show you what dye batch it came from. If you really run into trouble it is possible to use the yarn from the weaving in ends. Horrible thing to do, but possible and may just help if you are nearly there and only need a few more inches. Never waste yarn if you can help it and avoid throwing your cut off ends away until you are finished.

**Finding Help** The best place to ask for help is online at Ravelry.com. There are many groups on Ravelry who are willing to help. And you can get pattern support from the author in the same way.

# Glossary

**Acrylic** A synthetic yarn spun from polymer to resemble wool or other organic yarns. Hardwearing and lightweight.

**Amigurumi** A type of crochet accredited to the Japanese style of working in a continuous spiral (although work can be joined). The rate of increase and decrease of stitches creates shape, and originated from the Japanese style of dolls and animals with large heads and disproportionately small bodies.

**Back Loop** The back loop of the V loop when the work is facing you.

**Blocking** A method of stretching and resting a piece of crochet with the application of steam or water. The crocheted piece will then take on its proper shape.

**Cluster** A number of stitches worked together at the top, normally at the last part of the stitch.

**Cotton** A natural fibre made from the cotton plant.

**Edging** A decorative number of rows to finish off the item made. May or may not match the actual main fabric.

**Fasten Off** To finish the work, a final stitch is made, the loop drawn through, and yarn end cut.

**Felting** A method of washing a pure wool so that the fibres become matted and the piece shrinks considerably.

**Foundation Chain** This is the beginning chain, which lays the foundation on which the rest of the pattern will be formed.

**Free loop** These are unused loops left on parts of the top or bottom of the stitch in the previous row.

**Front Loop** The front loop of the V loop when the work is facing you.

**Gauge** An American term referring to the tension of the project.

**Hook** The thin metal, wooden or bamboo hook used to create crochet. Available in many sizes from 0.4 mm upwards.

**Join-as-you-go** A method of joining one motif to another while crocheting the last round.

**Mercerised Cotton** A chemical process that heats and shrinks cotton in such a way that it gives the cotton a sheen. The cotton is also stronger and resistant to mildew.

**Motif** A separately made piece, normally decorative, that is often repeated and joined to another to form part of a pattern.

**Picot** A number of chain stitches made and then joined with a slip stitch, usually to the first chain made, and which makes a little pointed bobble.

**Ply** The number of threads in yarn indicate its ply. A double knit (DK) is an 8-ply yarn.

**Pompom** A fluffy ball made in yarn. Used to decorate items.

**Post** This term is applied to the long part of the stitch.

**Right side** This is the side of the work that is facing you when you are working a row.

**Row** A section of the pattern that is either worked around or backwards/forwards.

**Seam** A join where two parts of crochet work are sewn together.

**Starch** An organic carbohydrate powder that is used to stiffen fabrics and laundry.

**Tension** The scale of the hook to yarn to pattern stitch that indicates to the maker that their finished item will finish to more or less the same size as that given in the pattern.

**Thread** A very fine yarn, usually cotton.

**Weaving In** Loose yarn ends are sewn carefully through the work in such a way that the ends are not visible, and the work does not loosen.

**Wool** Generally pure sheep's wool but also sometimes refers to any yarn that resembles real wool.

**Wraps Per Inch** A 2-dimensional measurement made by counting the number of times it is possible to wind the yarn or thread over a width of 1 inch. It helps to identify and compare thickness of yarns from different manufacturers.

**Wrong Side** The side of the work that is not visible in the finished item. (Except for Amigurumi where the wrong side of the work is the visible side.)

**Yarn** Wool, cotton, synthetic or mixed materials used in crochet.

# YARN INDEX

This index can help if you need to substitute a yarn.

| Yarn Name | Content | Ball/Skein Size | Yardage | Weight of Yarn/ Thread | WPI | Suggested Hook Size | Cleaning |
|---|---|---|---|---|---|---|---|
| Aida 5 Aida 10 Aida 15 (Coats) | 100% Mercerised Cotton | 50 g | 5: 200 (219 yds) 10: 265m (280 yds) 15: 330 m (361 yds) | 6 ply: weight 5, 10, 15 | N/A | 1.25–2 mm | Machine wash 95°C |
| Anchor Creativa Fino | 100% Mercerised Cotton | 50 g | 120 m (131 yds) | 4 ply | 14 | 2.5 mm | Machine wash at 40°C |
| ColourSpun | 100% Wool | 50 g | 100m (109 yds) | DK 8 ply | 10 | 4–4.5 mm | Hand wash cool |
| Patons 100 % Cotton 4 ply | 100% Mercerised Cotton | 100 g | 330 m (361 yds) | 4 ply | 14 | 3 mm | Machine wash 40°C |
| Patons Linen Touch DK | 74% Cotton 26% Linen | 50 g | 100 m (109 yds) | DK 8 ply | 11 | 4 mm | Machine wash 30° C. Gentle wash. Dry flat. |
| Peter Pan Cupcake | Nylon Acrylic | 50 g | 90 m (98 yds) | DK 8 ply | 11 | 4 mm | Machine Wash 40°C |
| Rico Creative Filtz | 100% Merino | 50 g | 50 m (104 yds) | Super Bulky | 5 | 8 mm | Hand wash cool |
| Rico Essential Cotton DK | 100% Mercerised Cotton | 50 g | 130 m (142 yds) | DK 8 ply | 14 | 3 mm | Machine wash 30°C |
| Rowan Belle Organic Aran | 50% Wool 50% Cotton Organic | 50 g | 90 m (98 yds) | Aran | 8 | 5 mm | Hand wash 30°C Dry Flat |
| Rowan Belle Organic DK | 50% Wool 50% Cotton Organic | 50 g | 120 m (131 yds) | DK 8 ply | 9 | 4 mm | Hand wash 30°C Dry flat |
| Rowan Big Wool | 100% Merino Wool | 100 g | 80 m (87 yds) | Super Bulky | 5 | 10-15 mm | Hand wash |
| Rowan Cotton Glace | 100% Cotton | 50 g | 115 m (125 yds) | Sport 5 ply | 12 | 3 mm | Machine wash 40°C Gentle. Dry flat |

| | | | | | | | |
|---|---|---|---|---|---|---|---|
| Rowan Fine Milk Cotton | 30% Milk Protein, 70% Cotton | 50 g | 150m (164 yrds) | 4 ply | 14 | 3 mm | Hand wash 30°C. Dry Flat. |
| Rowan Hand Knit Cotton | 100% Cotton | 50 g | 85 m (93 yds) | DK 8 ply | 10 | 4mm | Machine wash 40°C Gentle. Dry flat |
| Sirdar Country Style DK | 45% Acrylic 40% Nylon 15% Wool | 100 g | 318m (348yds) | DK 8 ply | 11 | 4mm | Machine Wash 40°C |
| Sirdar Snuggly Bamboo | 80% Bamboo 20% Wool | 50 g | 95 m (104 yds) | DK 8 ply | 11 | 4 mm | Warm wash. Do not iron. Reshape while wet. Minimum Machine Wash 40°C. |
| Stylecraft Special DK | 100% Acrylic | 100 g | 295m (322 yds) | DK | 11 | 4 mm | Machine Wash 40°C. |

**WPI: Wraps per inch** is the number of times the yarn can be wrapped over a 2.5 cm (1 in) length. The DK (8-ply) yarns vary from 9–14 wraps with the average being 11 WPI. In this book the finished size of the project is not critical in the same way as it is for garments, so you should be able to substitute yarn fairly easily.

**Suggested Hook Size:** This is not necessarily the hook size used in the patterns in this book, but rather the standard hook size recommended for this yarn.

**Care Instructions:** These are the care instructions given by the manufacturers, but always check the label first. For more information see Techniques.

## COMMON TERMS FOR THREADS/YARNS

| Standard Yarn Weight | UK term | Aus/NZ term | USA term | WPI (average) |
|---|---|---|---|---|
| 0 – Lace | Thread | 1-6-ply | Laceweight | 18+ |
| 1 – Superfine | 4-ply | 4-ply | Fingering/Sock | 14 |
| 2 or Fine | 5-ply | 5-ply | Sport | 12 |
| 3 or Light | DK | 8-ply | DK | 11 |
| 4 or Medium | Aran | 10-ply | Worsted | 9–10 |
| 5 or Bulky | Chunky | 12-ply | Bulky | 7 |
| 6 or Super bulky | Super chunky | Super bulky | Less than 100 | 5–6 |

(Source: www.ravelry.com)

# Information, Inspiration, Stockists and Suppliers

## JOIN A COMMUNITY

The internet has been largely responsible in helping the interest in crochet go global. One of the best tools around is a social networking site called Ravelry (www.ravelry.com).

Join the site for free, set up an Avatar name and create project pages with your own personal notes. You can also search for and buy patterns, create an online library and many other useful tools. There are groups to join. It is a helpful place to get help or to help others. Many groups do CAL (Crochet-a-Long) where you get to make something as part of a group – a great way to try new projects and extend your skill. Sharing your finished projects online is very satisfying as other members will give kind and generous feedback. Best of all, you make friends and find inspiration all around the world.

## BLOGGING INSPIRATION

There are plenty of crochet blogs to read. Below are blogs recommended by the author. They often have step-by-step tutorials and patterns, but most importantly may provide you with inspiration and ideas.

accordingtomatt.blogspot.co.uk Matt and Denis are two guys who crochet amazingly colourful things.

annemarieshaakblog.blogspot.co.uk A Dutch and English site with many inspirational tutorials and patterns – a European viewpoint.

attic24.typepad.com Probably the most famous crochet blog on the internet run by a housewife and mum who loves to share her colourful crochet with you. Tutorials are available.

calicoliving.blogspot.co.uk Author's blog with lifestyle articles about living well and creating a warm, lively and colourful home. Things to make, decorating tips and of course crochet is also there.

decor8blog.com A very popular interior decorating and styling blog with plenty of interesting ideas. Includes prolific writing and a good source of inspiration if you want to learn to display and style your home.

dottieangel.blogspot.co.uk Vintage-style crochet projects available. Helpful instruction with lots of inspiration.

dutchsister-s.blogspot.co.uk Interesting and inspiring things to make, many of which are crochet.

meme-rose.blogspot.co.uk Pretty crochet blog, with intense use of colour and feminine designs.

theroyalsisters.blogspot.co.uk Michelle designs some vintage country-style crochet based on the granny square. Plenty of free patterns and an interesting take on retro crochet.

## SHOP LOCAL

Many local yarn stores create small communities where you can meet and learn from other people. Below is a list of shops recommended by members of the Ravelry online community (www.ravelry.com).

Many of the shops offer workshops and classes and most have websites where you can order online. Some companies have more than one store and many also offer haberdashery products.

**Abakhan** has several stores including Stoke-on-Trent, Manchester, Liverpool and Wales.
Tel +44 (0)1745 562133
www.abakhan.co.uk

**All the Fun of the Fair**
2.8 Kingly Court, Carnaby Street, Soho
London, W1B 5PW
Tel +44 (0)7905 075017
www.allthefunofthefair.bigcartel.com

**Attica Yarns**
Unit 10b, Top Land Country Business Park
Cragg Vale, Hebden Bridge
West Yorkshire, HX7 5RW
Tel +44 (0)1422 884885

**Calon Yarns**
380 Cowbridge Road, Canton
Cardiff, Wales, CF5 1JJ

Tel +44 (0) 2920 211508
www.calonyarns.co.uk

**Create**
Victorian Arcade
South Hawksworth Street, Ilkley
West Yorkshire, LS29 9DY
Tel +44 (0)1943 817788
www.createcafe.co.uk

**Knit Nottingham**
91 Mansfield Road
Nottingham, NG1 3FN
Tel: +44 (0)115 947 4239
www.knitnottingham.co.uk

**Knitcraft**
25 Fore Street, Pool, Redruth
West Cornwall, TR15 3DZ
Tel +44 (0)1209 216661

**Lighthouse Yarns**
St George's Square
Belfast
Tel +44 (0)7825 140537

**Loop**
15 Camden Passage
London, N1 8EA
Tel +44 (0)207 288 1160
www.loopknitting.com

**McAree Bros** has several stores including Falkirk and Stirling.
19 Howe Street

Edingburgh, Scotland, EH3 6TE
Tel +44 (0)131 558 1747
www.mcadirect.com

Nest
102 Weston Park, Crouch End
London, N8 9PP
Tel +44 (0)208 340 8852
www.handmadenest.co.uk

Norfolk Yarns
288 Aylsham Road, Hellesdon, Norwich
Norfolk, NR3 2RG
Tel +44 (0)1603 417 001
www.norfolkyarn.co.uk

Ribbon Circus
8 Albert Street, Hebden Bridge,
West Yorkshire, HX7 8AH
Tel +44 (0) 1422 847803
www.ribboncircus.com

Yarn on the Square
22 Market Place, Ely
Cambridgeshire, CB7 4NT
Tel +44 (0) 1353 661 024

The Wool Baa
83 Junction Road, Sheffield
South Yorkshire, S11 8XA
Tel +44 (0)1142 666 262
www.thewoolbaa.co.uk

REPUBLIC OF IRELAND
Springwools

The Olde Sawmills, Ballymount Road
Walkinstown, Dublin 12 Republic of Ireland
Tel +35 31 450 9134
www.springwools.com

AUSTRALIA
Woolbaa
124 Bridport Street
Albert Park, VIC, 3206
E: sales@woolbaa.com.au
Tel +61 3 9690 6633
www.woolbaa.com.au

Spotlight
Tel 1300 305 405
http://spotlight.com.au

Lincraft
www.lincraft.com.au
Tel 1300 54627238

Bendigo Wollen Mills
4 Lansell St
Bendigo, VIC, 3550 Australia
Tel +61 3 5442 4600
www.bendigowoollenmills.com.au

The Wool Shack
PO Box 743 Inglewood, Perth, WA, 6932
www.thewoolshack.com
Tel +61 8 9371 8864

NEW ZEALAND
Spotlight
Tel 0800 276 222

www.spotlight.co.nz

Knit World
PO Box 30645
Lower Hutt 5040 New Zealand
Tel +64 4 586 4530
www.knitworld.co.nz

## GENERAL
HobbyCraft Group also has stores countrywide and sells books, yarns, and needlecraft notions. www.hobbycraft.co.uk

John Lewis plc has stores throughout the UK and stocks many brands of yarn as well as haberdashery. www.johnlewis.com

## ONLINE STORES
Purlescence specialises in luxury yarns and a fantastic range of wooden hooks.
www.purlescence.co.uk
Tel +44 (0)1865 589 944

Texere – art yarn supplier and shop.
www.texere-yarns.co.uk
Tel +44 (0) 1274 722 191

## YARN MANUFACTURERS
(Rowan, Aida, Patons and Anchor)
Coats Crafts UK
Green Lane Mill Holmfirth
West Yorkshire, HD9 2DX United Kingdom
Tel + 44 (0) 1484 681 881
www.knitrowan.com | www.coatscrafts.co.uk

Sirdar
Sirdar Spinning Ltd
Flanshaw Lane Wakefield
West Yorkshire, WF2 9ND United Kingdom
Tel + 44(0)1924 371 501
www.sirdar.co.uk

Stylecraft Yarns
PO Box 62
Goulbourne Street Keighley
West Yorshire, BD21 1PP United Kingdom
Tel +44(0) 1535 609 798
www.stylecraft-yarns.co.uk

Rico Design Gmbh & Co KG
Industrie str 19–23 33034 Brakel Germany
Tel + 49 (0)52 72602 0
www.rico-design.de

Colourspun
PO Box 2 Heidelberg , 1438
Republic of South Africa
Tel +27(0) 16 349 2949
www.colourspun.co.za

Peter Pan
Thomas B Ramsden
Netherfield Road
Guiseley
Leeds, LS20 9PD
United Kingdom
Tel + 44(0) 1943 872 264
www.tbramsden.co.uk

# Index

To my Ouma, Christina Pretorius.
My inspiration, determination and strength.

## Acknowledgements

Firstly my thanks go to the yarn suppliers for their very generous support. Their yarns have been lovely to work with and have allowed me to push my creativity and experiment freely. A big thank you to Mollie for letting me turn her living room into a workshop for months, and to other friends who helped in other ways, most notably Barry. Thanks goes for the very great patience of my editors, Simona, Clare and Lliane, New Holland Publishers for believing in the project and for giving me the chance to write this book in uncertain times. The biggest thank you goes to Murielle, Trenly, Megan and Tess whose love and belief was felt every step of the way. Thank you so much.

## About the Author

Natalie was taught to crochet when she was a little girl by her grandmother Christina Pretorius, sparking her interest in handicrafts and design. Natalie works as an interior designer, writer and furniture designer. She is passionate about lifestyle and, in particular about how we create our home environments.
Natalie lives in Cambridgeshire, England.
You can find Natalie on Ravelry as well as through her website
www.natalieclegg.co.uk